Beginning Perl Programming

From Novice to Professional

William "Bo" Rothwell

Apress®

Beginning Perl Programming: From Novice to Professional

William "Bo" Rothwell
San Diego, CA, USA

ISBN-13 (pbk): 978-1-4842-5054-9   ISBN-13 (electronic): 978-1-4842-5055-6
https://doi.org/10.1007/978-1-4842-5055-6

Managing Director, Apress Media LLC: Welmoed Spahr
Acquisitions Editor: Steve Anglin
Development Editor: Matthew Moodie
Coordinating Editor: Mark Powers

Cover designed by eStudioCalamar

Cover image designed by Freepik (www.freepik.com)

Distributed to the book trade worldwide by Springer Science+Business Media New York, 233 Spring Street, 6th Floor, New York, NY 10013. Phone 1-800-SPRINGER, fax (201) 348-4505, e-mail orders-ny@springer-sbm.com, or visit www.springeronline.com. Apress Media, LLC is a California LLC and the sole member (owner) is Springer Science + Business Media Finance Inc (SSBM Finance Inc). SSBM Finance Inc is a **Delaware** corporation.

For information on translations, please e-mail editorial@apress.com; for reprint, paperback, or audio rights, please email bookpermissions@springernature.com.

Apress titles may be purchased in bulk for academic, corporate, or promotional use. eBook versions and licenses are also available for most titles. For more information, reference our Print and eBook Bulk Sales web page at http://www.apress.com/bulk-sales.

Any source code or other supplementary material referenced by the author in this book is available to readers on GitHub via the book's product page, located at www.apress.com/9781484250549. For more detailed information, please visit http://www.apress.com/source-code.

Printed on acid-free paper

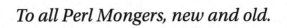

To all Perl Mongers, new and old.

Table of Contents

About the Author

At the impressionable age of 14, **William "Bo" Rothwell** crossed paths with a TRS-80 Micro-computer System (affectionately known as a "Trash 80"). Soon after, the adults responsible for Bo made the mistake of leaving him alone with the TRS-80. He immediately dismantled it and held his first computer class, showing his friends what made this "computer thing" work. Since this experience, Bo's passion for understanding how computers work and sharing this knowledge with others has resulted in a rewarding career in IT training. His experience includes Linux, Unix, DevOps tools, orchestration, security, and programming languages such as Perl, Python, Tcl, and BASH.

Bo can be contacted via LinkedIn: `www.linkedin.com/in/bo-rothwell`

About the Technical Reviewer

Germán González-Morris is a polyglot Software Architect/Engineer with 20+ years in the field, with knowledge in Java(EE), Spring, Haskell, C, Python, and Javascript, among others. He works with web distributed applications. Germán loves math puzzles (including reading Knuth) and swimming. He has tech reviewed several books, including an application container book (Weblogic), as well as titles covering various programming languages (Haskell, Typescript, WebAssembly, Math for coders, and regexp). You can find more details at his blog site (`https://devwebcl.blogspot.com/`) or twitter account (`@devwebcl`).

Acknowledgments

Thanks to all of the folks at Apress for helping me get this book to print:

- Steve: Thanks for getting the ball rolling.

- Matthew: Appreciate your "behind the scenes" guidance.

- Mark: Great job keeping this project on track.

- Germán: Excellent work finding my typos and technical oversights and bloopers.

Introduction

In the world of programming, there are many choices when it comes to languages. Each language has its advantages and disadvantages. No single language will fit all needs.

You may already know why you want to learn Perl 5. If that is the case, just dive right into this content. If you are still wondering why Perl 5 is a great language, then I would like to take a few moments to provide you with some good reasons, hopefully without any negative comments toward other languages.

Perl 5 is a very robust language that includes a great number of features that you would expect from a modern language. It is also easy to learn initially because there isn't a need for so much extra syntax that you commonly find in more structured languages.

Perl 5 also has a huge following with great documentation and online support. There are hundreds of thousands of Perl programs available, providing you with a great starting point whenever you start a new project. Many organizations have used Perl 5 for over two decades, making it very much embedded in the corporate IT world.

I hope you enjoy this book and that it helps you on journey of learning this fun and powerful language.

CHAPTER 1

Origin of Perl

Perl was developed in 1987 by Larry Wall. It was created because the tools that were available to Mr. Wall at the time (sed, C, awk, and Bourne shell) didn't provide the sort of functionality that he required.

Perl was initially called Pearl, but the name was quickly changed due to the fact that there was another language called Pearl at the time. Perl is a backronym (a constructed acronym created to fit an existing word) that stands for "Practical Extraction and Reporting Language." Some programmers (typically those who don't like Perl) claim that Perl stands for "Pathologically Eclectic Rubbish Lister."

Perl code is mostly machine-independent. This means that you can write a Perl program on one platform (like Linux) and then easily use the same program on another platform (like Windows). When dealing directly with the operating system or filesystem, you may need to make some changes to your code.

Perl has been ported to UNIX, Windows, Linux, and many others (see `www.cpan.org/ports` for the complete list).

Perl Development Environments

In some cases you might not have a choice as to which platform or derivative of Perl that you will use to develop your code. However, if you do have a choice, you should spend some time learning the differences between your options.

© William "Bo" Rothwell of One Course Source, Inc. 2019
W. "Bo" Rothwell, *Beginning Perl Programming*, https://doi.org/10.1007/978-1-4842-5055-6_1

*nix/Windows

*nix refers to any UNIX-based OS (including Linux). Many developers prefer this environment over Windows for several reasons, including the following:

- UNIX-based systems typically have more powerful features for developers. For instance, most UNIX-based systems have a C or C++ compiler, making it easier to install CPAN modules. Windows systems typically don't have a C/C++ compiler by default.

- UNIX-based systems tend to be more stable than Window-based systems.

There are other advantages (and some would argue there are advantages of Windows over *nix). Consider the pros and cons of each before deciding your development platform.

In either case, if you are worried about writing portable code, you probably want to review the following document: `http://perldoc.perl.org/perlport.html`.

Which Derivative for *nix?

If you decide to develop on a UNIX-based platform, you may want to consider which derivative of Perl to install and develop on. Unless you want to create a custom build of Perl (well beyond the scope of this book*), your choice will likely come down to two: the standard Perl derivative (`www.perl.org`) or ActiveState's ActivePerl (`www.activestate.com/activeperl`).

When you consider which derivative to use, take the following into account:

- Most *nix systems have Perl installed by default as several system tools (especially on Linux) make use of Perl to manipulate data. In these cases, you are likely to find the standard Perl installed (or a custom build for that Linux distribution).

- ActivePerl comes with a tool to easily install Perl modules: **ppm**. This tool is normally considered easier to use than installing CPAN modules with the -**MCPAN** option.

- ActivePerl's **ppm** doesn't install modules directly from CPAN, but rather from another repository that ActiveState maintains. This means you have access to a subset of the CPAN modules, not the complete set. Note: You can choose additional repositories by clicking "Edit" + "Preferences" and choosing the "repositories" tab.

*If you do want to create your own custom Perl derivative, you probably want to start by looking at the following: http://search.cpan.org/dist/App-perlbrew/.

Which Derivative for Windows?

If you are working on a Windows platform, you have a few choices available, as described on www.perl.org:

- **ActiveState Perl**: It has binary distributions of Perl for Win32 (and Perl for Win64).

- **Strawberry Perl**: A 100% Open Source Perl for Windows that is exactly the same as Perl everywhere else; this includes using modules from CPAN, without the need for binary packages (see http://strawberryperl.com/).

- **DWIM Perl for Windows**: A 100% Open Source Perl for Windows, based on Strawberry Perl. It aims to include as many useful CPAN modules as possible. It even comes with Padre, the Perl IDE (see http://dwimperl.szabgab.com/windows.html).

A few things to consider:

- ActivePerl has **ppm**, while Strawberry Perl does not. However, Strawberry Perl has many CPAN modules installed by default (both a pro and a con).

- With ActivePerl you can get official support. Strawberry Perl provides only community support.

- Strawberry Perl comes with **gcc**, a C/C++ compiler, making it easier to install modules from CPAN.

- Strawberry Perl release cycle tends to be slower than ActivePerl.

- "When I'm on Windows, I use Strawberry Perl."——Larry Wall

Pick Your Perl Development Tools

There are several good tools to help you develop your Perl code. This includes debuggers, editors, and IDEs. Some of these tools are free, while some can be very expensive. Many of them are community support, while a few are commercially supported.

A good place to start exploring these tools is the following web site: `www.perlmonks.org/?node_id=531175`.

Perl Versions

To verify Perl is installed, and to show the version, type the command **perl -v**:

```
[student@ocs student]$ perl -v

This is perl, v5.10.1 built for MSWin32-x86-multi-thread
(with 4 registered patches, see perl -V for more detail)

Copyright 1987-2009, Larry Wall

Binary build 1008 [294165] provided by ActiveState http://www.ActiveState.com
Built Dec  9 2010 06:00:35

Perl may be copied only under the terms of either the Artistic License or the
GNU General Public License, which may be found in the Perl 5 source kit.

Complete documentation for Perl, including FAQ lists, should be found on
this system using "man perl" or "perldoc perl".  If you have access to the
Internet, point your browser at http://www.perl.org/, the Perl Home Page.
```

You will see in the preceding highlighted text that Perl 5.10.1 is used on this system. As of the date of when this was written, this version is considered a bit "old"; however, it is important to note that many Perl developers are still using older versions. They may be "stuck" with an older version because of platform issues or "related" software issues. This book isn't written for a specific version of Perl 5; however, notes will be made when a "newer" concept is covered.

Perl 5.10.1 is specifically used in this book in some examples because of a change that took place in that version. Please note that all of the content in this book works on the latest version of Perl, unless otherwise noted.

What About Perl 6?

This book is based on Perl 5, which will prompt some readers to wonder about Perl 6. To begin with, Perl 5 and Perl 6 have some major differences. It would be difficult to cover both in the same book.

Perl 6 also has some excellent new features, many of which have been backported into Perl 5. However, Perl 6 hasn't been embraced by Perl developers to the extent that it overtakes Perl 5 in popularity. There are several theories as to why, but the most likely is the work that it would take to convert the vast number of Perl 5 scripts into Perl 6 scripts. The benefits of Perl 6 don't appear to outweigh the work involved to move to Perl 6 (although some would argue this isn't the case).

In any event, there is certainly a huge amount of Perl 5 development, and based on ongoing projects, this accounts for more development than on Perl 6. One day this will change, but for now Perl 5 is still heavily used.

Even if you plan on learning Perl 6, knowing Perl 5 will be useful as you may be called upon to upgrade existing Perl 5 scripts to Perl 6. As a result, consider learning more about Perl 6 by visiting this site: `http://perl6.guide/`.

Understanding Perl Versions

Perl version numbers sometimes are confusing. The first version of Perl 5 (5.000) was released in 1994. Initially, the Perl version numbers followed the numbering convention of 5.000, 5.001, 5.002, etc. When a minor change or "bug fix" release occurred, the numbering included this as 5.002_**001** or 5.002_**002**.

The last release that followed this convention was 5.005_63; the next release was 5.6.0. The primary reason for this numbering change was to fall in line with the version numbering system that most open source projects followed.

Additionally, odd number releases (5.7, 5.9, 5.11, etc.) are considered development releases and should not be used for "real" programming.

Previous release: 5.005_63	
Development releases	**Production releases**
	5.6
5.7	5.8
5.9	5.10
5.11	5.12
5.13	5.14
5.15	5.16
5.17	5.18
5.19	5.20

Note   The most current release as of when this book was written is 5.28.

Which version of Perl 5 should you use? In some cases you may not have a choice as your organization may have a specific version of Perl that you must use. However, if the choice is yours, consider the following:

- Newer versions have more features than older versions.

- Only the latest version and the previous production release are supported. Any older version is no longer actively maintained.

This book was specifically written to address subtle differences in different Perl 5 versions. Most of the material should work fine in Perl 5.6 and higher. When there are differences, they will be called out.

TRY IT!

Whenever you program in Perl, it is very helpful to know what version of Perl you are using. Execute the following command to determine the version of Perl that you are currently using:

```
perl -v
```

Invoking Perl

There are three methods to invoke Perl: the command line, interactive, and script methods.

The Command Line Method

Although this method is the least common way of invoking Perl, it does provide a means of "testing" simple Perl statements. The **-e** option allows the user to enter the Perl statements on the command line:

```
[student@ocs student]$ perl -e 'print "This is my first perl program\n";'
This is my first Perl program
```

Notes:

- The **print** statement will display its arguments to STDOUT (standard output, usually the screen).

- The "\n" character represents a newline character.

- The ";" character ends the **print** statement.

- The single quotes around the Perl statement are needed to "protect" special characters from the shell.

- The double quotes are needed around the text that will be printed by the **print** statement.

- In the Win32 environment, use double quotes around the **print** and single around the text.

The Interactive Method (Debugger)

The interactive method makes use of the Perl debugger to allow you to enter a Perl "shell" in which you can type Perl statements. This is useful not only for testing Perl scripts but also for "interactively" testing Perl statements.

To enter the Perl debugger, use the **-d** option:

```
[student@ocs student]$ perl -d -e "1;"
DB<1>
```

Notes:

- The **-e** option allows you to enter the Perl statement(s) on the command line. The "1;" is a "dummy" statement that has no real meaning (but provides Perl with valid code in order to enter the debugger).

- Instead of specifying **-e "1;"** you could specify a script name to debug the script.

- Many of the examples given in this book are performed within the debugger. This allows the instructor to demonstrate a concept or technique without having to create a full program.

- There are a (very) few statements/features that don't work in the Perl debugger.

If you installed Active State's ActivePerl, you might end up in their GUI-based debugger. To temporarily change your system to use the built-in Perl debugger, enter the following command(s) in your shell:

- Windows:

```
set PERL5DB=BEGIN { require 'perl5db.pl'; }
set PERLDB_OPTS=
```

- Linux, Unix, and macOS systems:

```
export PERLDB_OPTS=
```

To re-enable the PDK debugger, set the PERL5DB variable to an empty string.

 TRY IT!

Execute the following command to enter the Perl debugger environment:

`perl -d -e "1;"`

At the debugger prompt, execute the following Perl statement:

`print 5 + 6;`

Exit the debugger by executing the following Perl statement:

`q`

The Script Method

This method is the most common method; it allows you to place Perl statements inside of a file and execute them. The following line of text can be placed into a file:

#1_first.pl
```
print "This is my first Perl program\n ";
```

And then executed by using the Perl command:

```
[student@ocs student]$ perl 1_first.pl
This is my first Perl program
[student@ocs student]$
```

Note that the # character is for commenting and lines starting with it won't be processed by Perl (with the exception of shbang, as we'll see next).

Unix-based operating systems provide you another method of executing the script. You can place a special line of code at the top of the script called "shbang" (or "shebang") that tells the OS which command to use to execute the script.

The first line in the following script is shbang. It must start with "#!" and then contain the path to the command that will execute the script:

```
#!/usr/bin/perl
```
 # 1_second.pl
```
print "This is my second Perl program\n ";
```

Now that shbang has been added, just make the script executable and run it like a program:

```
[student@ocs student]$ chmod a+x 1_second.pl
[student@ocs student]$ ./1_second.pl
This is my second Perl program
[student@ocs student]$
```

Notes:

- On a Windows system, shbang is primarily treated as a comment (unless you use **#!perl** followed by an option to Perl). The Win32 environment uses file extension association (associating the ".pl" extension with the Perl Command Line Interpreter).

- The actual location of Perl may vary from one platform to another. The rest of the example in this book will use #!perl instead of attempting to guess the full path to the Perl executable.

Perl Documentation

One of the great features of Perl is the quality of its documentation. This documentation can be accessed from several different sources. One of these sources is the website `https://perldoc.perl.org`. While browsing this site, there are a few things that you want to take into consideration (see Figure 1-1).

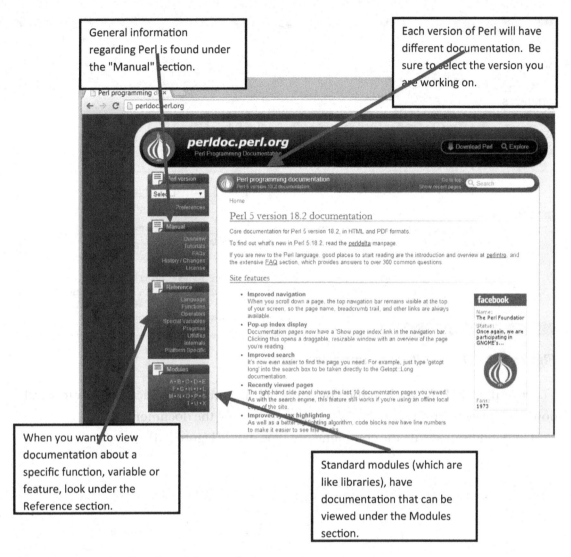

General information regarding Perl is found under the "Manual" section.

Each version of Perl will have different documentation. Be sure to select the version you are working on.

When you want to view documentation about a specific function, variable or feature, look under the Reference section.

Standard modules (which are like libraries), have documentation that can be viewed under the Modules section.

Figure 1-1.   *Details of perldoc.perl.org*

In addition to the web-based documentation, you can access documentation on your one system. If you are working on Unix or Linux, you can execute the command man perl (see Figure 1-2).

```
PERL(1)                    Perl Programmers Reference Guide                    PERL(1)

NAME
       perl - The Perl language interpreter

SYNOPSIS
       perl [ -sTtuUWX ]          [ -hv ] [ -V[:configvar] ]
            [ -cw ] [ -d[t][:debugger] ] [ -D[number/list] ]
            [ -pna ] [ -Fpattern ] [ -l[octal] ] [ -0[octal/hexadecimal] ]
            [ -Idir ] [ -m[-]module ] [ -M[-]'module...' ] [ -f ]
            [ -C [number/list] ]        [ -S ]        [ -x[dir] ]
            [ -i[extension] ]
            [ [-e|-E] 'command' ] [ -- ] [ programfile ] [ argument ]...

GETTING HELP
       The perldoc program gives you access to all the documentation that
       comes with Perl.  You can get more documentation, tutorials and
       community support online at <http://www.perl.org/>.

       If you're new to Perl, you should start by running "perldoc perlintro",
       which is a general intro for beginners and provides some background to
       help you navigate the rest of Perl's extensive documentation.  Run
       "perldoc perldoc" to learn more things you can do with perldoc.
Manual page perl(1) line 1
```

Figure 1-2. *The results of running* man perl

Press the "ENTER" key to scroll down one line at a time, the "space bar" key to scroll down one page at a time, and the "q" key to quit viewing the document.

On Windows, execute the command perldoc perl (Figure 1-3).

```
                         Command Prompt - perldoc perl                        _  □  x
NAME
    perl - Practical Extraction and Report Language

SYNOPSIS
    perl [ -sTtuUWX ] [ -hv ] [ -V[:*configvar*] ]
    [ -cw ] [ -d[t][:*debugger*] ] [ -D[*number/list*] ]
    [ -pna ] [ -F*pattern* ] [ -l[*octal*] ] [ -0[*octal/hexadecimal*] ]
    [ -I*dir* ] [ -m[-]*module* ] [ -M[-]*'module...'* ] [ -f ]
    [ -C [*number/list*] ] [ -P ] [ -S ] [ -x[*dir*] ] [ -i[*extension*] ]
    [ [-e|-E] *'command'* ] [ -- ] [ *programfile* ] [ *argument* ]...

    If you're new to Perl, you should start with perlintro, which is a
    general intro for beginners and provides some background to help you
    navigate the rest of Perl's extensive documentation.

    For ease of access, the Perl manual has been split up into several
    sections.

  Overview
        perl                    Perl overview (this section)
        perlintro               Perl introduction for beginners
        perltoc                 Perl documentation table of contents

        ActivePerl              ActivePerl overview

  Tutorials
        perlreftut              Perl references short introduction
        perldsc                 Perl data structures intro
-- More --
```

Figure 1-3. `perldoc perl` *on Windows*

Note   You can also execute the **perldoc** command on UNIX and Linux systems; however, the **man** command doesn't exist on Windows systems (unless additional software is installed).

If you review the main documentation page (https://perldoc.perl.org), you will discover many other useful sub-categories. The following highlights a few that you many consider taking the time to read through.

Document	Description
perlintro	Perl introduction for beginners
perlrequick	Perl regular expressions quick start
perlretut	Perl regular expressions tutorial
perlstyle	Perl style guide
perlcheat	Perl cheat sheet

Document	Description
perltrap	Perl traps for the unwary
perldebtut	Perl debugging tutorial
perlsyn	Perl syntax

Each of these can be viewed by either using the **man** command or the **perldoc** command. For example, to see the Perl cheat sheet, execute the **perldoc perlcheat** command.

TRY IT!

Execute the following command to display the "perl style guide":

```
perldoc perlstyle
```

To see documentation on a specific built-in function, use the -f option with the perldoc command. For example, to view the documentation for the Perl print function, execute perldoc -f print (Figure 1-4).

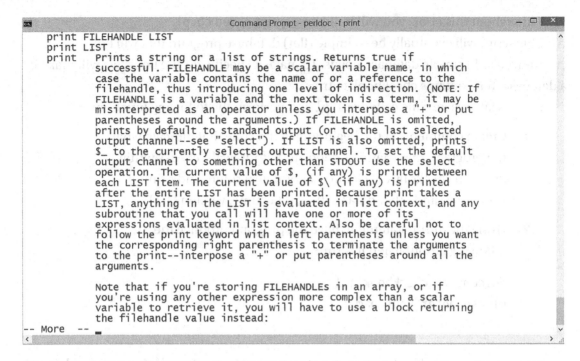

Figure 1-4. *Documentation for the Perl print function*

Perl Resources

In each chapter, resources are provided to provide the learner with a source for more information. These resources may include downloadable source code or links to other books or articles that will provide you more information about the topic at hand.

Resources for this chapter can be found here:

```
https://github.com/Apress/beginning-perl-programming
```

Lab Exercises

A note about the lab exercises in this book: creating lab exercises that will be beneficial to everyone can be difficult. Lab exercises that focus on specific scenarios (such as engineering test cases) can result in difficulties for learners who do not perform this sort of programming. As a result, I focused on creating labs that will perform tasks that are fairly generic but also assist the learner in practicing the new skills learned in each chapter. In addition, to make the lab exercises more realistic, I attempt to build on one script throughout rather than build many small scripts.

Throughout this book, you will build on a script called cb.pl.

This script will eventually be a simple (flat) database program that will be customized to fit simple database needs. To make it specific for the book, we will make it a database that contains checkbook entries.

For this lab, create a file called cb1.pl and perform the following functions:

1. Create comments at the beginning of the code that indicate what the program does (handles deposits, withdrawals, checks writing, looks up checks by check number or date written, and prints a statement) and other data (author, date/time, version (1.1)).

2. Using the print statement, have the program produce the following output when it is run:

```
Welcome to checkbook 1.1
Please enter your name:
```

When you have completed your work, compare your script against the cb1.pl file provided in the lab answers.

CHAPTER 2

Scalar Variables

Numeric Literals

A numeric literal is simply any kind of valid number. In Perl the following numeric types are supported:

- Integer (ex: 111)

- Floating point (1.11)

- Hex (0x111)

- Octal (0111)

- Scientific (1.11E3)

While it's important to know what numeric types Perl supports, it's also important to understand that Perl doesn't "treat" these types differently. In fact, all numbers (and strings) are considered to be of one type in Perl: scalar.

Also note that while you can represent scalar values as Hex, Octal, or Scientific, Perl will really treat them as integer values:

```
  DB<1> print 0x111
273
  DB<2> print 0111
73
  DB<3> print 1.11E3
1110
```

Scalar data is "a single value." This could be any of the preceding numeric "formats" or any string (strings are discussed later in the chapter).

© William "Bo" Rothwell of One Course Source, Inc. 2019
W. "Bo" Rothwell, *Beginning Perl Programming*, https://doi.org/10.1007/978-1-4842-5055-6_2

Manipulating Numbers

There are three basic types of operations you can perform on numbers: mathematical, predefined functions, and comparison. Numeric comparison will be discussed in a later chapter when all types of comparisons are covered.

Mathematical Operations

Perl allows the following mathematical operations:

Operation	Symbol	Example	Result/Notes
Addition	+	6+5	11
Subtraction	−	10-6	4
Multiplication	*	2*8	16
Division	/	20/8	2.5
Modulus (remainder)	%	20%8	4
Exponentiation	**	2**5	32
Auto-increment	++	See later section.	Note: The auto-increment and auto-decrement operators can only be used on scalar variables (not on constant numbers).
Auto-decrement	−−	See later section.	

Examples:

```
  DB<1> print 3 * 8
24
  DB<2> print 2 ** 5
32
```

Predefined Functions

Perl has some useful predefined functions that can be used to manipulate numbers (more modern versions of Perl also support trigonometry functions, such as **sin** and **cos**).

Operation	Function	Example	Result
Absolute value	abs	abs(-101)	101
Convert hex to integer	hex	hex("f0")	240
Integer value	int	int(12.98)	12
Convert octal to integer	oct	oct("0570")	376
Generate random (floating point) number	rand	rand(10)	Varies depending upon random seed
Square root	sqrt	sqrt(100)	10
Set random seed	srand	srand(200)	N/A

Examples:

```
  DB<1> print hex("e2")
226
  DB<2> print int(101.02)
101
```

Note   The **rand** and **srand** functions are discussed in detail in a later chapter.

 TRY IT!

Execute the following command to enter the Perl debugger:

```
perl -d -e "1;"
```

Execute the following commands in the Perl debugger to practice math operations:

```
print 5 * 5;
print 10 / 0;
```

```
print sqrt(9);
```

Exit the Perl debugger by executing the following debugger command:

```
q
```

String Literals

A string literal is a set of characters that have quotes (double or single) surrounding them. Some examples of strings are as follows:

> "a is the first letter of the alphabet"

> "John is late for work"

> 'Perl is the best programming language in the world'

Notes:

- There is a difference between single and double quotes which will be discussed in a later section.

- Even though strings are created by placing quotes around characters, it is important to note that what really makes something a string is the function or operator that is performed on the value. This will be covered in greater detail in a later section of this chapter.

Manipulating Strings

As with numbers, there are three basic types of operations you can perform on strings: alteration operators, predefined functions, and comparison operators. String comparison will be discussed in a later chapter when all types of comparisons are discussed.

Alteration Operators

There are two alteration operations you can perform on strings.

Operation	Symbol	Example	Result
Concatenate	.	"abc"."def"	abcdef
Repeat	x	"abc"x5	abcabcabcabcabc

Why use the **x** operator? Consider the following example:

```
DB<1> print "-" x 30, "\n", "Name: Bob Smith\n", "-" x 30
------------------------------
Name: Bob Smith
------------------------------
```

Predefined Functions

Here are some predefined functions:

Operation	Function	Example	Result
Delete newline character at end of string	chomp	See later section of this chapter	N/A
Delete last character of string	chop	See later section of this chapter	N/A
Return index of substring	index or rindex	See later chapter	N/A
Merge multiple strings together	join	See later chapter	N/A
Turn all CAPS to lowercase	lc	lc("HELLO")	hello
Turn first char to lowercase	lcfirst	lcfirst("HELLO")	hELLO
Returns the length of the string	length	length("abc")	3
Break string into elements (array)	split	See later chapter	N/A
Returns a substring of a string	substr	See later chapter	N/A
Turn all lowercase to CAPS	uc	uc("hello")	HELLO
Turn first char to CAPS	ucfirst	ucfirst("hello")	Hello

Notes:

- **chomp** and **chop** will be discussed in more detail in a later section of this chapter because they are more commonly used on variables, not string constants.

- **index**, **rindex**, **join**, **split,** and **substr** will be discussed in a later chapter.

 TRY IT!

Execute the following command to enter the Perl debugger:

```
perl -d -e "1;"
```

Execute the following commands in the Perl debugger to practice string operations:

```
print "Bob" . "Smith";
print "Bob" . " " . "Smith";
print length("Bob");
```

Exit the Perl debugger by executing the following debugger command:

```
q
```

The Importance of Using Quotes

Perl is often referred to as a "lazy" programming language as it sometimes allows you to omit some syntax. For example, consider the following code:

```
DB<1> $var=red
DB<2> print $var
red
```

In the previous code, the value of red should have had quotes around it. However, it seems to have worked just fine without the quotes. Unfortunately, that won't always be the case.

When Perl sees a value without quotes around the value, it assumes initially that this is a function call. If there actually is a function called red, the function would be called, and the *return value* of the function would be assigned to the $var variable:

```
DB<1> sub red {return "haha";}        #creates a function called red
DB<2> $var=red
DB<3> print $var
haha
```

Only if red isn't a function would it be considered a scalar value. As a result, it is always safer to place quotes around the value:

```
$var="red";
```

Strings vs. Numbers

While numbers and strings are both scalar data to Perl, they are sometimes treated differently (depending on how they are used).

When numbers are used in a "string context," they are converted into strings first and then "used." String context includes the following:

- String operators ("." or "x")

- String functions (see preceding function)

- Assignment operation (the = sign)

- String comparison (described in a later chapter)

- Regular expressions (described in a later chapter)

The method Perl uses to convert numbers into strings is very simple. Essentially, the number is treated as if there were quotes around it. The only time the number is modified is when it contains unnecessary "0"'s after the decimal point. They are dropped when the number is used as a string.

Examples:

```
DB<1> print "abc".12345
abc12345
DB<2> print "abc".123.45
```

abc123.45
  DB<3> **print "abc".123.4500**
abc123.45

The string to number conversion is a bit more complex. Perl will "look" at the first character of the string and...

- ...if it is a number (0-9) or a decimal point, then Perl will continue to look for more numbers. Once it finds a character that is not either a number or decimal point, it will stop looking and will convert the string into what it has found to that point.

- ...if it is white space (new line, space, tab, etc.), Perl will ignore it and look at the next character to determine if it is a number, decimal point, or non-number.

- ...if it isn't a number, decimal point, or white space, then the string is treated as zero (0).

Examples:

  DB<1> **print "123abc"+10**
133
  DB<2> **print "   123abc"+10**
133
  DB<3> **print "abc123" +10**
10
  DB<4> **print "1.45 xyz" + 10**
11.45

Perl is also smart enough to know that a number can't have two decimal points. Once a second decimal point is discovered, Perl stops looking and treats all characters to that point as the number:

  DB<1> **print "9.999.999" + 10**
19.999

The Assignment Operation

It is important to remember that the assignment operation is string. This may sometimes pose problems:

```
DB<1> $num=120.4500000
DB<2> print $num
120.45
```

In the previous example, we tried to assign a very precise number to the variable $num. However, because the assignment operation is string, the "unnecessary" zeros were removed from the number. In most cases this isn't a problem, but if you want to show how precise the number really is, this is a disadvantage.

To avoid this, use quotes around the number:

```
DB<1> $num="120.4500000"
DB<2> print $num
120.4500000
```

Note that this does not make $num into a variable that holds a string. It is a scalar variable, not a numeric or string variable. If you use a numeric operator or function on the variable, then it will be treated as a number; if you use a string operator or function on the variable, then it will be treated as a string.

 TRY IT!

Execute the following command to enter the Perl debugger:

```
perl -d -e "1;"
```

Execute the following commands in the Perl debugger to test the difference between strings and numbers:

```
print "1000 monkeys" + 5;
print length(123.45000);
print "work" / "time";
```

Did you get the results that you expected? If not, review the last section and determine why the output was different than you expected.

Exit the Perl debugger by executing the following debugger command:

```
q
```

Single vs. Double Quotes

Quotes are important when dealing with strings because they tell Perl how to handle the strings.

Double Quotes

There are many "special characters" that you can have within double quotes. These characters are called "escape characters" because the escape key (\) is used to create them:

Escape character	Meaning
\t	Tab
\n	Newline character
\r	Return
\u	Makes the next character uppercase
\l	Makes the next character lowercase
\U	Makes all following characters uppercase
\L	Makes all following characters lowercase
\E	Ends the \U and \L modifications
\f	Form feed
\b	Backspace
\a	Bell
\033	Octal character
\x1b	Hex character
\"	Double quote

Examples:

```
DB<1> print "It is a good idea to learn Perl\n"
```
It is a good idea to learn Perl

```
DB<2> print "hello\t\t\tgoodbye"
```
hello   goodbye
```
DB<3> print "hello\b\b\b\b\bgoodbye"
```
goodbye
```
DB<4> print "The \Usign\E said \Ustop\E\n"
```
The SIGN said STOP

Within double quotes, "$" and "@" are also special characters. The "$" character is used to specify a scalar variable, while the "@" character is used to specify an array variable. Variable dereferencing (returning the value that is assigned to the variable) takes place within double quotes:

```
DB<1> $code="A127Z"    #sets a scalar variable
DB<2> print "The code is $code"
```
The code is A127Z

If you want to print double quotes within a double-quoted string, you need to put an escape character (backslash) preceding the double quotes:

```
DB<1> print "The key word is \"test\""
```
The key word is "test"

Single Quotes

Almost all of the characters within single quotes are treated as plain characters. The only special characters within single quotes are single quotes and (sometimes) escape characters:

```
DB<1> print 'Bob's new car is broken'
```
Substitution replacement not terminated at (eval 4)[C:/Perl/lib/perl5db.
pl:1521] line 2.
```
DB<2> print 'The last character is \'
```
Can't find string terminator "'" anywhere before EOF at (eval 5)[C:/Perl/
lib/perl5db.pl:1521] line 2.

In order to have a single quote within a single-quoted string, you must put an escape character before it:

```
DB<1> print 'Bob\'s new car is broken'
Bob's new car is broken
```

Since an escape character before a single quote makes it into a plain character, you need to escape the escape character in such cases:

```
DB<1> print 'The last character is \\'
The last character is \
```

Within single quotes, the escape character has no special meaning in front of other characters, and the $ character is just a plain character:

```
DB<1> print 'The result is 10\n'
The result is 10\n
DB<2> print 'The total is $total'
The total is $total
```

 TRY IT!

Execute the following command to enter the Perl debugger:

```
perl -d -e "1;"
```

Execute the following commands in the Perl debugger to practice how single and double quotes are different:

```
print "Hello there\tBob; how are\nyou today?";
print 'Hello there\tBob; how are\nyou today?';
```

Exit the Perl debugger by executing the following debugger command:

```
q
```

Scalar Variables

A "scalar value" is a single item of data. This data can consist of characters that are found in the ASCII text table. Scalar variables are used to store scalar values. The "$" character is used to specify a variable name:

$var=value;

The variable name ($var in the preceding example) can contain alpha characters (lower- and uppercase), numbers, and underscore characters. It must also start with an alpha character or an underscore character. While some Perl built-in variables can start with a numeric character, the variables that you create cannot start with a numeric character.

To dereference the value a variable contains, specify the variable's name:

```
DB<1> $test=94
DB<2> print "The result of the test is $test"
The result of the test is 94
```

Undefined Variables

If you attempt to reference a variable that has not been defined, Perl does not consider this an error. The value that Perl returns depends upon how the variable is being used. In numeric operations, Perl will return 0; in string operations, Perl will return "" (null string):

```
DB<1> print "The name of the car is $name"
The name of the car is
DB<2> print "The value is: " , $total + 8
The value is: 8
```

Note   The comma used in the second example separates the string from the mathematical operation. This sequence of items separated by commas is called a **list** in Perl.

In some cases, you don't want to perform an operation if a variable isn't defined. The **defined** function can be used to check if a variable is defined or not. If the variable is defined, **defined** returns a "true" value; if the variable isn't defined, **defined** returns a "false" value.

These values can be used in conditional statements. In a later chapter, we will discuss conditional statements in detail. The following code is just a brief example:

```
#!perl
#2_defined.pl

if (defined ($total)) {
    print "The value is: ", $total +8, "\n";
}
else
{
    print 'The variable $total is not defined', "\n";
}
```

Notes:

- The **if** statement will be discussed in detail in a later chapter. In this example, the first **print** statement is executed if $total is defined. The second **print** statement is executed if $total is not defined.

- The curly braces { } define a "block" of statements. Blocks are required for conditional statements to tell Perl what statements to execute if the condition is true (or false in the case of the **else** portion).

To "undefine" a variable that has been defined, use the **undef** function:

```
DB<1> $total=95
DB<2> print "The total is $total\n"
The total is 95
DB<3> undef ($total)
DB<4> if (defined ($total)) { \
cont:    print "yes\n";              \
cont: } else {                       \
cont:    print "no\n";            \
cont: }
no
```

Notes:

- The outcome of the **if** statement will be to print "no" since $total is not defined.

- Setting a variable to "" or 0 does not "undefine" it.

- In the Perl debugger, the statement is automatically executed after you press the "Enter" key. To continue the command, type a backslash character right before the "Enter" key. This is the purpose of the backslash characters that are use with the **if** statement in the previous example.

 TRY IT!

Execute the following command to enter the Perl debugger:

```
perl -d -e "1;"
```

Execute the following commands in the Perl debugger to practice setting and unsetting variables:

```
if (defined $person) {print "yes"};
$person="Nick";
if (defined $person) {print "yes"};
undef $person;
if (defined $person) {print "yes"};
```

Exit the Perl debugger by executing the following debugger command:

```
q
```

Auto-increment and Auto-decrement

As mentioned previously, the "++" and "--" operators can be used to alter numeric variables. The ++ (auto-increment) operator will add 1 to the variable. The "--" (auto-decrement) operator will subtract 1 from the variable.

Examples:

```
DB<1> $i=100
DB<2> $i++
DB<3> print "$i"
101
DB<4> ++$i
DB<5> print $i
102
```

The difference between **$i++** and **++$i** is when the incrementing takes place. For example, the following will add 1 to $a and then assign that new value to $b:

```
DB<1> $a=10
DB<2> $b=++$a
DB<3> print $a
11
DB<4> print $b
11
```

If the operator occurs after the variable, then the original value is first returned (and, in this case, assigned to the $b variable) and then the variable is incremented:

```
DB<1> $a=10
DB<2> $b=$a++
DB<3> print $a
11
DB<4> print $b
10
```

Warning   Don't use auto-increment or auto-decrement on variables that contain strings. As mentioned previously, Perl will (normally) try to convert the string into a number. Often this results in a "logical error":

```
DB<1> $name="Bob Smith"
DB<2> $name++
DB<3> print $name
1
```

In this example, Perl treats "Bob Smith" as the number 0, then adds 1 to 0 and reassigns $name to the value of 1.

Perl Magic with the Auto-increment Operator

The Perl documentation on the auto-increment operator includes the following statement:

The auto-increment operator has a little extra built-in magic to it. If you increment a variable that is numeric, or that has ever been used in a numeric context, you get a normal increment. If, however, the variable has been used in only string contexts since it was set, and has a value that is not the empty string and matches the pattern /^[a-zA--Z]*[0-9]*\z/ , the increment is done as a string, preserving each character within its range, with carry

This fancy description is meant to describe the following behavior:

```
DB<1> $name="Bob"
DB<2> $name++
DB<3> print $name
Boc
```

A simpler way of describing this behavior is that if the variable contains only alphanumeric characters (and not just numeric characters), then the auto-increment operator will increase the value of the "string" by one (based on the ASCII text table).

Note   The point behind this isn't to encourage you to use this feature, but rather to make you aware of this "Perl magic" in the event you come across some code that makes use of this feature.

To increment or decrement a variable by a different value than 1, use this technique:

```
DB<1> $a=100
DB<2> $a+=5
DB<3> print $a
105
DB<4> $a-=20
DB<5> print $a
85
```

This method also allows the use of multiplication and division:

```
DB<1> $a=20
DB<2> $a*=3
DB<3> print $a
```
60
```
DB<4> $a/=6
DB<5> print $a
```
10

✄ Cool Trick   You can append a string to an existing string variable by using the following:

```
$var .= "string";
```

 TRY IT!

Execute the following command to enter the Perl debugger:

```
perl -d -e "1;"
```

Execute the following commands in the Perl debugger to practice variable modification with the operators that were covered in this section:

```
$total=1000;
$total++;
print $total;
$result=++$total;
print "$total and $result";
$total *=3;
print $total;
```

Exit the Perl debugger by executing the following debugger command:

```
q
```

Reading Data from the User

There are several methods of reading input:

- The standard input filehandle

- The diamond operator (discussed in a later chapter)

- User-created filehandles (discussed in a later chapter)

The most common method of reading input is the *standard input filehandle.*
A filehandle is a connection between your script and a "port." The standard input
filehandle reads data from the port connected to standard input (usually data coming
from the keyboard, but this data could also come from a file or the output of another
process).

<STDIN> represents the standard input filehandle. In the following example, the
user should be prompted to provide their age via the keyboard. Whatever the user types
is placed in the $age variable:

```
print "Please enter your age:";
$age=<STDIN>;
```

chomp and chop

When data is read from <STDIN>, the data that is stored in the variable includes **all**
the characters that are typed by the user. For example, consider if a user were asked for
his/her age and the user provides the data displayed in bold here:

```
  DB<1> print "Please enter your age: "; $age=<STDIN>
Please enter your age: 35
```

So, in this example, $age will store the string "35\n". Why "\n"? Because the user had
to press the Enter (or Return) key after typing "35". The Enter key, "\n", is also stored in
the variable. Since this extra character often causes problems, it is useful to know how to
get rid of it.

To verify that there actually is a newline character in the variable, consider the following output:

```
  DB<1> print "Please enter your age: "; $age=<STDIN>
Please enter your age: 35
  DB<2> print length($age)
3
  DB<3> print "You are $age years old"
You are 35
 years old
```

There are two Perl statements you can use to eliminate extra character from the end of a string: **chop** and **chomp**.

The chop Statement

The **chop** statement will remove (and return) the last character of a string:

```
$var="Now is a good time to buy stock\n";
chop $var;                          #chops off new line character
print chop $var;                    #chops off "k" and returns
                                    #value to print statement

$char=chop $var;                    #chops off "c" and returns
                                    #value to assignment
```

The chomp Statement

The **chomp** statement will only remove newline characters at the end of a string:

```
$var="Now is a good time to buy stock\n";
chomp $var;                         #chomps off new line character
```

When you know that you only want to remove a newline character, it is safer to use the **chomp** statement. When you want to remove any character, then the **chop** statement is better.

✹ **Cool Trick**   You can receive input and use the **chomp** statement at the same time using the following syntax:

```
chomp($name=<STDIN>);
```

 TRY IT!

Execute the following command to enter the Perl debugger:

```
perl -d -e "1;"
```

Execute the following commands in the Perl debugger to practice dealing with user input:

```
$person=<STDIN>;
print $person . " " . print length($person);
chomp $person;
print $person . " " . print length($person);
chomp $person;
print $person . " " . print length($person);
chomp $person;
print $person . " " . print length($person);
```

Exit the Perl debugger by executing the following debugger command:

```
q
```

Curly Braces

Consider the following code:

```
DB<1> $name="Bob"
DB<2> print "$name would rather be called $nameby"
Bob would rather be called
```

The intended output of this script is

```
Bob would rather be called Bobby
```

Unfortunately, this script will result in a logical error. Perl will return the value of the $nameby variable (when what is really wanted is the value of the $name variable and "by" to be treated as plain text). Because this variable doesn't exist, Perl returns a null string.

To avoid this, place curly braces around the variable name:

```
DB<1> $name="Bob"
DB<2> print "$name would rather be called ${name}by"
Bob would rather be called Bobby
```

The curly braces tells Perl that the variable name is $name and that the string "by" is just plain text.

Additional Resources

In each chapter, resources are provided to provide the learner with a source for more information. These resources may include downloadable source code or links to other books or articles that will provide you more information about the topic at hand.

Resources for this chapter can be found here:

```
https://github.com/Apress/beginning-perl-programming
```

Lab Exercises

Important Note   If you did not finish the previous lab, either finish it before starting this lab or use the completed cb1.pl provided in the code download.

Edit the file called cb1.pl and perform the following enhancements (save the changes into a file called cb2.pl):

- Have the user's name read into a variable called $name.

- Have the user's current balance printed (Note: Hard code the current balance to be "100" for now) followed by this menu:

  1. Enter a deposit

  2. Enter a withdrawal

3.   Enter a check

4.   Lookup a check by #

5.   Lookup a check by date

6.   Print a statement

7.   Exit program

Please enter your menu option:

- Have your script prompt the user for their menu choice and assign the input to a variable called $choice (don't forget to chomp off the newline character).

When you have completed your work, compare your script against the cb2.pl file provided in the lab answers.

CHAPTER 3

Array Variables

Array Variables

Array variables are used to store lists (groups) of scalar data. The following describes important information about array variables:

- The variable starts with a "@" symbol (not a $ symbol like scalar variables).

- The variable name rules (start with an alpha or underscore character, use only alphanumeric & underscore chars) for scalar variables also apply to array variable names.

- Array sizes don't have to be declared; Perl dynamically takes care of the size of the array.

- Individual scalar data within the array are referred to as "elements."

- An element can be treated as either a string or number.

To create an array, use the following syntax:

```
@colors=("red", "blue", "green");
```

Note   The value on the right-hand side of the = operator is called a list. A list is generated by placing a series of scalar values, separated by commas, within a set of parenthesis. This list is the data structure that an array holds.

© William "Bo" Rothwell of One Course Source, Inc. 2019
W. "Bo" Rothwell, *Beginning Perl Programming*, https://doi.org/10.1007/978-1-4842-5055-6_3

Referencing Array Elements

To reference an element in an array, use the following syntax:

```
print "$colors[0] is the color name in the list\n";
```

Array elements are indexed by integers (starting from 0). Therefore, the first element is element "0", the second element is element "1", and so forth.

The most confusing aspect of referring to an element is the use of the "$" character. Why "$" and not "@"?

Think of it this way: "@" is used to indicate array data and "$" is used to indicate scalar data. An element of an array **is** scalar data (a single value); therefore, when referring to it, use a "$" character.

If you wanted to print the entire array (or a portion of it), you would use the "@" symbol:

```
print "@colors";
```

Note   Without the quotes (""), all of the elements would be printed "Mashed together".

Some other referencing examples:

```
print "$colors[1] \n";          #prints the second element in the array.

print "@colors[1..3]\n";        #prints from the second to the fourth
element in the #array.

print "@colors[1,3]\n";         #prints from the second and the fourth
element in #the array.

print "$colors[$#colors] \n";   #prints the last element in the array
                                ($#arr holds the #last index number of the
                                array "arr").

print "$colors[-1]\n";          #prints the last element in the array
                                (alternative method).

print "$colors[99]\n";          #prints the 100th element in the array. If not
                                #defined, prints "" (0 in numeric situations)
```

$# what?

For each array, there is a scalar variable ($#array_name) that stores <u>the index number</u> of the last element. For example, a 5 element array called "@students" has a corresponding scalar variable called "$#students" which contains the value 4.

Warning   Don't change this scalar variable. Changing the $# variable of an array will change the size of the array, including possibly removing elements from the array!

Typically you should avoid changing the $# variable of an array directly. Perl will automatically change this as more elements are added or removed from the array. If you do make changes to this variable, you may end up losing data:

```
DB<1> @colors=("red", "blue", "green", "yellow", "purple")
DB<2> print "@colors"
red blue green yellow purple
DB<3> print $#colors
4
DB<4> $#colors=2
DB<5> print "@colors"
red blue green
```

One situation in which you may want to modify the $# variable is if you want to remove a bunch of elements from the end of the array. For example, the following line would permanently delete the last 20 elements from the @colors array:

```
$#colors -= 20;
```

TRY IT!

Execute the following command to enter the Perl debugger:

```
perl -d -e "1;"
```

Execute the following commands in the Perl debugger to practice creating and referencing elements in an array:

```
@names=("Bob", "Sue", "Nick", "Fred", "Ted");
print "@names";
print $names[0];
print $names[-1];
print $#names;
```

Exit the Perl debugger by executing the following debugger command:

```
q
```

Adding and Removing Elements in an Array

You can use built-in functions or a "manual method" to add and remove elements in an array. The built-in functions are as follows.

push	Add new element to end of array
unshift	Add new element to beginning of array
pop	Remove (and return) last element of array
shift	Remove (and return) first element of array

Function examples:

```
@flowers=("rose",  "tulip");          #creates the array flowers.

push(@flowers, "daisy");              #puts daisy at end of array.

unshift(@flowers, "carnation");       #puts carnation at beginning
                                      #of array.

pop (@flowers);                       #removes last element (daisy).
```

44

```
$plant=pop(@flowers);                    #removes last element (tulip) and
                                         #assigns it to the variable $plant.

shift(@flowers);                         #Removes the first element (carnation)
```

 TRY IT!

Execute the following command to enter the Perl debugger:

```
perl -d -e "1;"
```

Execute the following commands in the Perl debugger to practice adding and removing elements in an array:

```
@names=("Bob", "Sue", "Nick", "Fred", "Ted");
print "@names";
push (@names, "Tim");
unshift (@names, "Todd");
print "@names";
$last=pop (@names);
$first=shift (@names);
print "@names";
print $last;
print $first;
```

Exit the Perl debugger by executing the following debugger command:

```
q
```

To manually add elements in an array, assign the array to "itself" **and** the elements you wish to add:

```
@flowers=(@flowers, "daisy");            #puts daisy at end of array.

@flowers=("carnation", @flowers);        #puts carnation at beginning
                                         #of array.
```

To manually remove elements in an array, assign the array **and** a scalar variable (or value) to the array itself:

```
($plant, @flowers)=@flowers;          #Assigns @flowers to all but the
                                       #first element which is placed
                                       #in $plant.
```

The advantage of this method over statements like **pop**, **push**, **unshift,** and **shift** is that this method allows you to add and remove elements that are not either the first or the last element in an array:

```
#Following line inserts "daisy" after the fourth element of the array:
@flowers=(@flowers[0..3], "daisy", @flowers[4..7]);

#Following line removes the fourth element of the array:
@flowers=(@flowers[0..2], @flowers[4..$#flowers]);
```

However, for very large arrays, this method uses more memory and takes more time than the splice statement that is described in the next section.

The splice Function

You can also use the **splice** function to add or remove items from an array. With this function, the following syntax is used:

```
splice (ARRAY, OFFSET, LENGTH)
```

OFFSET is where you want to begin splicing from and LENGTH is how many elements to splice. For example, to remove the fourth element from an array, use this syntax:

```
DB<1> @colors=("red", "blue", "green", "yellow", "purple", "tan")
DB<2> splice (@colors, 3, 1)
DB<3> print "@colors"
red blue green purple tan
```

To replace one or more values in an array, you add the values to add at the end of the list of arguments. For example, to replace the fourth element with "teal", use this syntax:

```
DB<1> @colors=("red", "blue", "green", "yellow", "purple", "tan")
DB<2> splice (@colors, 3, 1, "teal")
DB<3> print "@colors"
```
red blue green teal purple tan

To insert a value into an array, you add the values to add at the end of the list of arguments. For example, to insert "teal" after the fourth element, use this syntax:

```
DB<1> @colors=("red", "blue", "green", "yellow", "purple", "tan")
DB<2> splice (@colors, 3, 0, "teal")
DB<3> print "@colors"
```
red blue green teal yellow purple tan

Note that the third argument is 0, meaning that none of the original elements will be replaced.

Why use the manual method that was shown in the previous section rather than the **splice** statement? The **splice** statement is quicker and takes less memory, but there are a couple of reasons why you want to know about the manual method:

- Older versions of Perl didn't have the **splice** statement, so if you are maintaining older Perl code, the manual method may be used. So, at the very least, you should at least be aware of this method.

- With the **splice** method, you can't insert or remove in more than one non-continuous place. With the manual method, you can do something like the following:

  ```
  @flowers=(@flowers[0..2], "daisy", @flowers[3..4], "rose",
  @flowers[5..7]);
  ```

TRY IT!

Execute the following command to enter the Perl debugger:

```
perl -d -e "1;"
```

Execute the following commands in the Perl debugger to practice using the splice statement:

```
@names=("Bob", "Sue", "Nick", "Fred", "Ted");
print "@names";
splice (@names, 2, 0, "Sally", "Steve");
```

```
print "@names";
$person=splice(@names, 3, 1);
print "$person";
print "@names";
```

Exit the Perl debugger by executing the following debugger command:

```
q
```

Using the for Loop

The idea behind looping through an array is to perform actions on each element on an array. In order to do this, you can use either a **for** or a **foreach** loop.

The **for** loop is a generic (not specifically for arrays) statement which has the following syntax:

```
for (initial statement; conditional evaluation; post statement) {
    statement(s);
}
```

The *initial statement* is done only once (when the **for** loop begins) and is usually used to assign a variable a starting value.

The *conditional evaluation* is done once at the beginning and each time after the *statement(s)* and *post statement* have been executed. Conditional evaluations are discussed in detail in the next chapter.

The *post statement* is executed after the *statement(s)* have been executed. It is usually used to increment or decrement the variable that was set with the initial statement.

In the following example, the **for** loop will print a countdown from 20 to 1:

```
for ($i=20; $i > 0; $i--) {
    print "$i\n";
}
```

In this example, the **for** loop will print out each element of an array on a separate line:

```
@arr=("north", "south", "east", "west");
for ($i=0; $i <= $#arr; $i++) {
    print "$arr[$i]\n";
}
```

Using the foreach Loop

The **foreach** loop is really just a modified form of the **for** loop. The syntax for the **foreach** loop is

```
foreach $var (@array) {
    statement(s);
}
```

The *$var* is a scalar variable that will hold each of the elements of an array, one element at a time. Each time through the loop, the variable $var contains the next element in the array.

The *@array* is the array to loop through.

The following code will print out each element of an array (like the preceding example) using the **foreach** loop:

```
@arr=("north", "south", "east", "west");
foreach $direction (@arr) {
    print "$direction\n";
}
```

Important Note   The name of the array **must** be within parentheses () in a **foreach** loop.

Be Careful of the Iterator Variable

The variable that is used to iterate the array is a special variable called a reference variable. Any changes that you make to this variable within the loop will result in changes to the array elements:

```
DB<1> @colors=("red", "blue", "green", "yellow", "purple")
DB<2> foreach $hue (@colors) {$hue="grey";}
DB<3> print "@colors"
grey grey grey grey grey
```

In addition, this variable is localized (it has scope), so the changes made to the iterator variable will not affect anything outside of the **foreach** loop:

```
DB<1> $hue="PURPLE"
DB<2> @colors=("red", "blue", "green", "yellow", "purple")
DB<3> foreach $hue (@colors) {$hue="grey";}
DB<4> print $hue
PURPLE
```

An Alternative to Using the for Statement

Often a traditional **for** statement can be replaced with a **foreach** loop:

```
DB<1> for ($i=1; $i <= 5; $i++) {print "$i\n";}
1
2
3
4
5
DB<2> foreach $i (1..5) {print "$i\n";}
1
2
3
4
5
```

The 1..5 creates a list of integers from 1 to 5 (1, 2, 3, 4, 5). The $i variable is assigned to these values one at a time.

TRY IT!

Execute the following command to enter the Perl debugger:

```
perl -d -e "1;"
```

Execute the following commands in the Perl debugger to practice using the foreach loop:

```
@names=("Bob", "Sue", "Nick", "Fred", "Ted");
foreach $person (@names) {print ++$count . "\t $person"};
foreach $person (@names) {$person .= " Smith";};
foreach $person (@names) {print "$person\n";};
```

Exit the Perl debugger by executing the following debugger command:

```
q
```

The reverse Statement

The **reverse** statement will assign the reverse of an array to another array:

```
@arr=("north", "south", "east", "west");
@revarr = reverse (@arr);
print "@revarr";                        #prints west east south north
```

In the preceding example, the array @arr is not modified. You can have the array itself modified by assigning the outcome of **reverse** to the original array:

```
@arr=("north", "south", "east", "west");
@arr = reverse (@arr);
print "@arr";                           #prints west east south north
```

The **reverse** statement can also be used on a scalar value to return the reverse of the scalar:

```
DB<1> $test="abc"
DB<2> $newtest=reverse $test
DB<3> print $newtest
cba
```

The sort Operator

The **sort** operator will perform an ASCII sort on the elements of an array:

```
@arr=("north", "south", "east", "west");
@sortarr = sort (@arr);
print "@sortarr";                    #prints "east north south west"
```

There are *many* other "types" of sorts that you can perform; for example, the following performs a numeric sort:

```
@num=(10,7,99,93,0);
@sortnum=sort {$a <=> $b} (@num);
print "@sortnum";            #prints 0 7 10 93 99
```

You must use $a and $b. Additionally, the order of $a and $b matter. If $a is first, then an ascending sort will occur. If $b is first, then a descending sort will occur:

```
  DB<1> @num=(10,7,99,93,0);
  DB<2> @sortnum=sort {$b <=> $a} (@num)
  DB<3> print "@sortnum"
99 93 10 7 0
```

Advanced sort Techniques

You can also perform operations on **$a** and **$b** before the sort takes place. A common example is to make a case-insensitive sort by using the **lc** (lowercase) function:

```
DB<1> @arr=("north", "south", "East", "West");
DB<2> @sortarr = sort (@arr);
DB<3> print "@sortarr";
East West north south
DB<4> @sortarr = sort { lc($a) cmp lc ($b) } (@arr);
DB<5> print "@sortarr";
East north south West
```

The **sort** is a lot more powerful than many Perl programmers realize. For example, suppose you had a list of files in an array and you want to sort them by file size:

```
@by_size=sort { -s $a <=> -s $b } @files;
```

There are many additional sorting techniques; however, many of them require you to have more knowledge about Perl. Consult the documentation for sort for more details.

TRY IT!

Execute the following command to enter the Perl debugger:

```
perl -d -e "1;"
```

Execute the following commands in the Perl debugger to practice using the sort statement:

```
@names=("Bob", "Sue", "Nick", "Fred", "Ted");
@sorted=sort(@names);
print "@sorted";
push (@names, "ned");
@sorted=sort(@names);
print "@sorted";
@sorted=sort { lc($a) cmp lc ($b)} (@names);
print "@sorted";
```

Exit the Perl debugger by executing the following debugger command:

```
q
```

The qw and qq Statements

The **qw** (quote words) statement will create a comma, quoted separated list from its arguments. It is primarily used as a short-hand method of creating lists. For example, the following array declaration...

```
@directions= ('n', 's', 'e', 'w', 'ne', 'nw', 'se', 'sw');
```

...can be rewritten using **qw** like this:

```
@directions=qw(n s e w ne nw se sw);
```

It is important to keep in mind that the values passed to the **qw** statement will be treated as if they were placed in single quotes. For example, if you pass variables, the variables will not be dereferenced:

```
DB<1> $name1="Bob"
DB<2> $name2="Sue"
DB<3> $name3="Tim"
DB<4> @names=qw($name1 $name2 $name3)
DB<5> print $names[0]
```
$name1

Note   If you want the strings to be double quoted, instead of single quoted, use the **qq** operator.

Arrays Used in Scalar Context

When you attempt to use an array when a scalar is supposed to be used, it is referred to as using an array in "scalar context."

The result of using an array in scalar context is that the number of elements in the array is returned, not the elements in the array. An example of using an array in scalar context is attempting to assign an array to a scalar variable:

```
DB<1> @names=("Bob", "Sue", "Ted")
DB<2> $people=@names
DB<3> print $people
```
3

While this may sometimes be beneficial, a better method of getting the number of elements of an array is to use the **scalar** statement:

```
DB<1> @names=("Bob", "Sue", "Ted")
DB<2> $people=scalar (@names)
DB<3> print $people
```
3

While the result is the same, the intention of the statement is much clearer.

Additional Resources

In each chapter, resources are provided to provide the learner with a source for more information. These resources may include downloadable source code or links to other books or articles that will provide you more information about the topic at hand.

Resources for this chapter can be found here:

```
https://github.com/Apress/beginning-perl-programming
```

Lab Exercises

Important Note   If you did not finish the previous lab, either finish it before starting this lab or use the completed cb2.pl provided in the lab answers folder.

Edit the file called cb2.pl and perform the following enhancements (save the changes into a file called cb3.pl):

- Create an array called @book that has the following string as the first element:

  "DEP:12/12/1999:Beginning Balance:100"

- Each element in the array will be one record which has four fields:

  Type_of_transaction:date_of_transaction:comment:amount_of_ transaction

When you have completed your work, compare your script against the cb3.pl file provided in lab answers.

CHAPTER 4

Associative Array Variables

Associative Array Variables

Consider the situation in which you are keeping track of dog names in an array:

@dogs=qw(Fido Spot Teddy Rex);

You also want to keep track of the owners of these dogs. One way we can do this is to create a second array:

@owners=qw(Bob Sue Fred Sally);

This, however, isn't the best solution. While not impossible, this method will be cumbersome because you will have to maintain two arrays (and carefully too!).

The problem with arrays is that the indexing system is already predefined.

@dogs		@owners	
Index	Value	Index	Value
0	Fido	0	Bob
1	Spot	1	Sue
2	Teddy	2	Fred
3	Rex	3	Sally

It would be nice if you could have the index be the owner's name and the value *associated* with that index be the dogs name...

© William "Bo" Rothwell of One Course Source, Inc. 2019
W. "Bo" Rothwell, *Beginning Perl Programming*, https://doi.org/10.1007/978-1-4842-5055-6_4

...and that is what associative arrays are all about.

%dog_owners	
Key (aka index)	**Value**
Bob	Fido
Sue	Spot
Fred	Teddy
Sally	Rex

Notes about associative arrays:

- Associative arrays are also called "hashes."

- Associative array variables start with a percent sign (%).

- The term index is used for regular arrays; the term "key" is used for associative arrays.

- The key/value pair is stored in a seemingly "random" order. Note the comment about this in the **perlsec** documentation guide (`http://perldoc.perl.org/perlsec.html#Algorithmic-Complexity-Attacks`):

  ...the algorithm used to "order" hash elements has been changed several times during the development of Perl, mainly to be reasonably fast. In Perl 5.8.1 also the security aspect was taken into account.

  In Perls before 5.8.1 one could rather easily generate data that as hash keys would cause Perl to consume large amounts of time because internal structure of hashes would badly degenerate. In Perl 5.8.1 the hash function is randomly perturbed by a pseudorandom seed which makes generating such naughty hash keys harder.

The last note causes some concern for first-time Perl programmers. It essentially means that when you ask for the keys/values of a hash, they are not returned in the same order that you created them in. Keep in mind that order is not the purpose of a hash, but rather the association between the key and the value is what hashes are all about. If you want order, use a regular array.

Creating Associative Arrays

There are two different (syntax) methods of creating an associative array. One method is a "quick and dirty" method that is easy to type, but difficult to read:

```
%dog_owners=qw(Bob Fido Sue Spot Fred Teddy Sally Rex);
```

The second method is more difficult to type, but easier to read:

```
%dog_owners=(
    "Bob"          =>      "Fido",
    "Sue"          =>      "Spot",
    "Fred"         =>      "Teddy",
    "Sally"        =>      "Rex"
);
```

As far as Perl is concerned, both methods are the same. The second method, while more difficult to create, is easier to read and understand by other programmers.

Note   The => is the same as a comma in Perl. In other words, you could create a regular array with the following syntax:

```
@colors=("red" => "blue" => "yellow");
```

The purpose of => is to provide a way to make it visually clear what value a key is "pointing to." So, while => can be used in place of a comma in any situation, you should *normally* use them for associate arrays.

To create an individual key/value pair, use the following syntax:

```
$dog_owners{"Nick"}="Mikey";
```

This technique can also be used to modify an existing value for a specific key:

```
$dog_owners{"Nick"}="Fido";
```

To access a value of a key, use the following syntax:

```
print "$dog_owners{Bob} is owned by Bob\n";
```

Note   While keys must be unique, values do not have to be unique.

 TRY IT!

Execute the following command to enter the Perl debugger:

```
perl -d -e "1;"
```

Execute the following commands in the Perl debugger to practice creating hashes and accessing hash data:

```
%phone=("Bob" => "555-1234", "Tim" => "555-7890");
print $phone{"Bob"};
$phone{"Bob"} = "555-9999";
print $phone{"Bob"};
$phone{"Sue"} = "555-7777";
print $phone{"Sue"};
```

Exit the Perl debugger by executing the following debugger command:

```
q
```

Accessing Values with keys and foreach

There are two methods of "looping" (accessing every key/value pair separately) though associative arrays: using a **foreach** loop or using a "**while-each**" loop. Each method has its advantage and disadvantage.

To use the **foreach** loop to loop through a hash, you first need to obtain all of the keys of a hash. The **keys** function will return all of the keys of an associative array. These keys are returned in a list format and can either be assigned to an array

```
@owners=keys (%dog_owners);
print "@owners";
```

or manipulated like an array:

```
foreach $person (keys %dog_owners) {
    print "$dog_owners{$person} is owned by $person\n";
}
```

Using keys on a Regular Array

As of Perl 5.12, you can use **keys** on an array to return the index values of an array:

```
  DB<1> print "@INC"
C:/Perl64/site/lib C:/Perl64/lib .
  DB<2> @test=keys (@INC)
  DB<3> print "@test"
0 1 2
```

Sorting the Output

Although the order that the keys are returned isn't the same order as the key/value pairs were created, it is possible to sort the values of the keys to produce an order:

```
  DB<1> %dog_owners=qw(Bob Fido Sue Spot Fred Teddy Sally Rex);
  DB<2> foreach $person (sort keys %dog_owners) { \
  cont:      print "$dog_owners{$person} is owned by $person\n"; \
  cont: }
Fido is owned by Bob
Teddy is owned by Fred
Rex is owned by Sally
Spot is owned by Sue
```

As mentioned previously, there are many different ways to sort a list. For example, the following will sort based on the values, rather than the keys:

```
  DB<1> %dogs=qw(Bob Fido Sue Spot Fred Teddy Sally Rex);
  DB<2> foreach $person \
  cont:    (sort { $dogs{$a} cmp $dogs{$b} } keys %dogs) { \
  cont:        print "$dogs{$person} is owned by $person\n"; \
  cont:    }
```

Fido is owned by Bob
Rex is owned by Sally
Spot is owned by Sue
Teddy is owned by Fred

Accessing Values in with "while-each" Loops

The disadvantage of using a **foreach** loop to loop through a hash is that a list is created when the **keys** statement is used. This is a disadvantage because it takes more memory to store this list and it takes time to create the list.

A more efficient method of looping through a hash is by using a combination of the **while** and **each** statements. The **each** statement will return a single key/value pair from the hash, starting with the first one found in memory. It will continue to return key/value pairs in "order" (based on how they are stored in memory) until there are none left. After the last key/value pair has been returned, the next **each** statement will return an empty list which is would be considered to be a value of false in a conditional statement.

A "while-each" loop doesn't create an extra array. Instead, it extracts key/value pairs one at a time and assigns them to scalar variables:

```
while (($key, $value) = each (%dog_owners)) {
    print "$value is owned by $key\n";
}
```

 TRY IT!

Execute the following command to enter the Perl debugger:

```
perl -d -e "1;"
```

Execute the following commands in the Perl debugger to practice looping through a hash:

```
%phone=("Bob" => "555-1234", "Tim" => "555-7890");
while (($person, $num) = each (%phone)) {print "$person = $num";};
```

Exit the Perl debugger by executing the following debugger command:

```
q
```

Be Careful While Using each

The disadvantage with a "while-each" loop is what takes place when the associative array is modified within the loop. Any modification of the associative array (adding key/value pairs, removing key/value pairs, or changing existing key/value pairs) can cause a "rehash." The documentation on each describes what happens when you change a hash and then use the **each** statement:

> If you add or delete a hash's elements while iterating over it, the effect on the iterator is unspecified; for example, entries may be skipped or duplicated--so don't do that. Exception: It is always safe to delete the item most recently returned by each(), so the following code works properly:

```
while (($key, $value) = each %hash) {
print $key, "\n";
delete $hash{$key}; # This is safe
}
```

Resetting the Iterator

Each hash has a separate iterator (how Perl keeps track of where it is in the hash when you are parsing through the elements using the while-each loop). You may want to reset the iterator manually. To do so, just execute the **keys** statement on the hash:

```
keys %hash;
```

This is useful when you reach a point where you want to stop parsing through the hash. A later while-each loop may start in the wrong location if you don't reset the iterator.

Note   Calling the **values** statement on a hash will also reset the iterator.

Using each on Arrays

As of Perl 5.12, you can use the **each** statement to iterate through an array:

```
DB<1> while (($index, $value) = each (@INC)) {\
cont:     print "$index - $value\n"; \
cont: }
0 - C:/Perl64/site/lib
1 - C:/Perl64/lib
2 - .
```

Returning Keys Only with each

When used in scalar context, each only returns keys:

```
DB<1> %dogs=qw(Bob Fido Sue Spot Fred Teddy Sally Rex);
DB<2> while ($key=each(%dogs)) {\
cont:     print "$key is a key\n"; \
cont: }
Sally is a key
Bob is a key
Sue is a key
Fred is a key
```

The values Statement

The **values** statement can be used to access just the values of the key/value pair:

```
@dogs=values (%dog_owners);
```

This can be useful if you want to find out how many dogs are named "Spot":

```
foreach $name (values (%dog_owners)) {
   if ($name eq "Spot") {
      $spot++;
   }
}
```

TRY IT!

Execute the following command to enter the Perl debugger:

```
perl -d -e "1;"
```

Execute the following commands in the Perl debugger to practice getting the values of a hash:

```
%phone=("Bob" => "555-1234", "Tim" => "555-7890");
@nums=values(%phone);
print "@nums";
```

Exit the Perl debugger by executing the following debugger command:

```
q
```

Reverse Searching an Associative Array

Unfortunately when you use values, there is no way to get the key associated with the value. To search for a key when given a value you can use a while-each loop:

```
#4_rev.pl

%dogs=qw(Bob Fido Sue Spot Fred Teddy Sally Rex);

while (($key, $value) = each (%dog_owners)) {
   if ($name eq $value) {
      print "$value is owned by $key\n";
   }
}
```

Notes:

- While keys are unique, values are not. Therefore, there could be more than one line of output in the preceding program.

- Once you find a match, you may want to stop looking. In a later chapter, the **last** statement is explained; **last** will allow you to prematurely exit loops.

Removing Associative Array Keys and Values

To remove both the key and value of an associative array, use the **delete** statement:

```
delete $dog_owners{Bob};
```

You can assign the items that are deleted to either scalar variables or to an array:

```
($key, $value) = delete $dog_owners{Bob};
@data = delete $dog_owners{Bob};
```

To remove the value, but keep the key, use the **undef** statement:

```
undef $dog_owners{Fred};
```

exists vs. defined

As we saw earlier, the **defined** statement can be used to determine if a scalar variable has been set:

```
if (defined ($total)) {
    print "The value is: ", $total +8, "\n";
}
else
{
    print 'The variable $total is not defined', "\n";
}
```

The **defined** statement can also be used to determine if a value of a key/value pair has been defined:

```
if (defined ($dog_owners{Nick})) {
    print "Nick has a dog\n";
}
else
{
    print "Nick doesn't have a dog\n";
}
```

While the **defined** statement is used to determine if the value has been set, the **exists** statement is used to determine if the *key* exists:

```
%dog_owners=(Bob, Fido, Sue, Spot, Fred, Teddy, Sally, Rex);

undef $dog_owners{Bob};

if (defined ($dog_owners{Bob})) {        #false in this case
   print "Bob has a dog\n";
} else {
   print "Bob doesn't have a dog\n";
}

if (exists ($dog_owners{Bob})) {         #true in this case
   print "Bob is a key in the array\n";
} else {
   print "Bob is not a key in the array\n";
}
```

 TRY IT!

Execute the following command to enter the Perl debugger:

```
perl -d -e "1;"
```

Execute the following commands in the Perl debugger to practice removing elements from a hash:

```
%phone=("Bob" => "555-1234", "Tim" => "555-7890", "Sue" => "555-9999");
while (($person, $num) = each (%phone)) {print "$person = $num";};
undef $phone{"Tim"};
while (($person, $num) = each (%phone)) {print "$person = $num";};
if (defined ($phone{"Tim"})) {print "yes";};
if (exists ($phone{"Tim"})) {print "yes";};
delete $phone{"Sue"};
while (($person, $num) = each (%phone)) {print "$person = $num";};
```

Exit the Perl debugger by executing the following debugger command:

```
q
```

Special Variables

Perl has special (often pre-set) variables. These variables may either contain data for the programmer's use or data that modifies how Perl behaves.

As this book progresses, some of these special variables will be introduced. However, keep in mind that while Perl has many special variables, a good deal of them require more advanced knowledge of Perl or are fairly esoteric.

Special variables have a unique naming convention. While normally you can't have a variable in Perl that starts with a non-alphanumeric (or underscore) character, special variables often start with one of these characters. As a result, you will find that many of the Perl special variables have names like $$, $|, and $(. Keep in mind that the first dollar sign character is used to indicate the type of variable (scalar in the case of $$, $|, and $( ), so the real names of these variables are $, |, and (.

The Environment Variables

Environment variables are stored by the operating system. They are normally used to modify how the user's OS environment works or to store information relating to the user's log in session.

Each OS has different environment variables. For example, there is an environment variable in Linux/UNIX called USER that stores the user's log in name. In DOS/Windows this variable is USERNAME.

These variables are passed into your script into an associative array called **%ENV**. The key is the name of the variable and the value is what the variable was set to.

Many of these variables are useless to the Perl programmer. Some, however, are very useful. To see what variables are set on your system, just run the following Perl script:

```perl
#!perl
#4_env.pl
foreach $var (keys %ENV) {
   print "Var: $var   Set to: $ENV{$var}\n";
}
```

The syntax for accessing a value of an environment variable is the same as any associative array:

```perl
print "Your log in name is $ENV{USER}\n";
```

TRY IT!

Execute the following command to display the environment variables on your system:

```
perl 4_env.pl
```

The Argument Variable

The @ARGV array contains the arguments passed into the Perl script. The first argument is stored in $ARGV[0], the second argument is stored in $ARGV[1], etc. In addition, the name of the Perl script that is being executed is stored in the $0 variable:

```perl
#!perl
#4_argv.pl
#This script adds up to three arguments and prints the result on the screen
$total=$ARGV[0] + $ARGV[1] + $ARGV[2];
print "$total\n";

print "This command is called $0\n";
```

Output example:

```
[student@ocs student]$ ./4_argv.pl 20 30 40
90
This command is called ./4_argv.pl
```

Notes:

- If only two arguments were passed into the script, then $ARGV[2] would be undefined and treated as "0" in the preceding program .

- The @ARGV array is no different than any other regular array other than it is pre-populated; This means you can treat it like an array and use any array statement (**sort**, **reverse**, **pop**, **push**, etc.) on @ARGV.

Additional Resources

In each chapter, resources are provided to provide the learner with a source for more information. These resources may include downloadable source code or links to other books or articles that will provide you more information about the topic at hand.

Resources for this chapter can be found here:

```
https://github.com/Apress/beginning-perl-programming
```

Lab Exercises

There won't be any need for hashes in the checkbook program that you have been creating, so this lab exercise will be for a standalone program. For this lab, create a menu-driven program that will allow a user to keep track of other people's phone numbers. This program should have the following choices:

1. Add a phone number

2. Lookup a phone number

3. Delete a phone number

4. Print all phone numbers

5. Check if a person has a phone number

6. Exit the program

Obviously you want this program to store this data in a permanent file. Unfortunately, we've not covered this topic (or conditional statements). So, a "starter" program has been created for you under the "Chapter_4-_Associate_Array_Variables" folder. Use start.pl to create your program (note the comments in the file that indicate where you need to place your code).

Some notes:

- Your hash should be called %phone.

- The lab answer provides some error checking. Whenever possible, perform error checking.

When you have completed your work, compare your script against the phone.pl script provided in the lab answers.

CHAPTER 5

Flow Control

Blocks

Control statements are used to handle conditional statements. A conditional statement is something that returns a value (true or false) based upon the current data available to your program.

For example, if the user running the program enters his/her age and this is stored in a variable called $age, we can check to see if $age is greater than 20 and then take some action based upon the outcome.

The following illustrates the different control statements we will cover in this chapter:

- if
- unless
- while
- until
- foreach
- for

A block is a grouping of statements that tells Perl what action(s) to take within a conditional statement. Placing curly braces { } around the statements forms the block.

The if Statement

The **if** statement is used to determine if something is true or false and to take action based upon this outcome. The syntax of the **if** statement is

```
if (condition) {
    if_statements;
}
```

© William "Bo" Rothwell of One Course Source, Inc. 2019
W. "Bo" Rothwell, *Beginning Perl Programming*, https://doi.org/10.1007/978-1-4842-5055-6_5

```
else {
    else_statements;
}
```

If the outcome of the *condition* is true, then the *if_statements* will be executed.

If the outcome of the *condition* is false, then the *else_statements* will be executed.

The following program will verify that the user's input (their age) is greater than 15:

```
#!perl
#5_age1.pl
print "Please input your age ";
$age=<STDIN>;
if ($age > 15) {
    print "You are old enough to drive\n";
}
else {
    print "You can't drive for ", 16 - $age, " more years\n";
}
```

Notes:

- <STDIN> is a filehandle which will read data from the keyboard and assign it to the variable $age.

- The else part of the **if** statements is optional.

- "True" in Perl is any number besides zero or any string besides "" (the empty string).

- The condition "$age > 15" is a numeric comparison. The next Chapter details other comparisons available in Perl.

TRY IT!

Execute the following command two times to demonstrate the use of the if statement:

`perl 5_age1.pl`

When prompted for the age the first time the program is executed, enter the following:

10

When prompted for the age the second time the program is executed, enter the following:

17

Using elsif

Suppose you want to modify the script from the previous page. If the person's age is greater than 15, then the output will be "You are old enough to drive".

Otherwise, we will do a second check and see if the person is exactly 15 years old. If they are, then the output will be "You are old enough for a permit".

Otherwise, the output will be "You can't drive for", 16 - $age, "more years".

```perl
#!perl
#5_age2.pl
print "Please input your age ";
$age=<STDIN>;
if ($age > 15) {
    print "You are old enough to drive\n";
}
elsif ($age == 15) {
    print "You are old enough for a permit\n";
}
else {
    print "You can't drive for ", 16 - $age, " more years\n";
}
```

Notes:

- The **elsif** condition will only be checked if the **if** condition is false.

- If both conditions are false, then the **else** block of the statement is executed.

One-Line if Statement

In keeping with Perl's "more than one way to do it" attitude comes the one-line **if** statement. Consider the following two sentences:

- If the trash is full, take it out.

- Take out the trash if it is full.

In both cases, the same message is conveyed. Perl allows the same "feature" with the **if** statement:

```
if ($x < 16 ) {
    print "too young to drive\n";
}

print "Too young to drive\n" if ($x < 16);
```

Both of the preceding examples produce the exact same result. Note that the second statement doesn't even need the parentheses around the conditional statement:

```
print "Too young to drive\n" if $x < 16;
```

TRY IT!

Execute the following command to enter the Perl debugger:

```
perl -d -e "1;"
```

Execute the following commands in the Perl debugger to see both regular if statements and one-line if statements in action:

```
$number=100;
if ($number == 100) {print "yes";};
print "yes" if $number == 100;
```

Exit the Perl debugger by executing the following debugger command:

```
q
```

The unless Statement

The **unless** statement is the logical opposite of the **if** statement:

```
unless (condition) {
  unless_statements;
}
else {
   else_statements;
}
```

If the outcome of the *condition* is **false**, then the *unless_statements* will be executed. If the outcome of the *condition* is **true,** then the *else_statements* will be executed.

Example:

```
print "Please input your age ";
$age=<STDIN>;
unless ($age < 16) {
   print "You are old enough to drive\n";
}
```

Note:

- There are some cases where **unless** is easier to read, but many times it just creates confusion. You can always use the **if** statement instead of the **unless** statement because you can "negate" the outcome of a conditional statement as you will see in a future Chapter.

The switch Statement

Prior to Perl 5.8, there was no switch (or case) statement available in Perl. In Perl 5.8, a *module* was added to provide this functionality.

The topic of using modules will be covered in more detail in a later chapter. In a nutshell, a module provides more functionality in your Perl scripts by importing functions or variables into your program. In this section, we will just focus on using the **switch** function that is provided by the **Switch** module.

The basic syntax of a **switch** statement is described in the following block:

```
switch (VAR) {
      case COND {STATEMENT(S) }
      case COND {STATEMENT(S) }
      else      {STATEMENT(S) }
}
```

In a real **switch** statement, VAR is replaced with a variable for evaluation. COND is replaced with a conditional statement (something that returns true or false), and STATEMENT(S) is/are replaced with what Perl code you wish to run if the COND is true.

Note that once a COND returns "true," no additional conditions are reviewed. In other words, only the first COND matches.

The **else** line is used in case no other lines match.

In the following example, the **switch** statement is used to determine if the user responds with "yes" or "no":

```
#!perl
#5_switch.pl

use Switch;  #Loads the switch module

print "Please enter 'yes' or 'no':";
$response=<STDIN>;
chomp $response;

switch ($response) {
        case "yes" {print "You agree!\n"; }
        case "no"  {print "Bummer, you don't agree\n"; }
        else       {print "Maybe next time\n"; }
}
```

Note   The Switch module exists in Perl 5.8-5.12. It does not exist in Perl 5.14+. This is due to the fact that in Perl 5.10, the **given** statement was added to the core functions with the intention of replacing the Switch module.

TRY IT!

Only if you are using Perl 5.8, 5.10, or 5.12, execute the following command to see a demonstration of the switch module:

```
perl 5_switch.pl
```

The given Statement

As of Perl 5.10, the **given** statement is available and designed to replace the **switch** statement. It is a feature that will be available in Perl 6 and has been "backported" to Perl 5. To make use of this Perl 6 feature in Perl 5, use the following syntax:

```
use feature "switch";
```

It is slightly confusing that asking for the "switch" feature gives you access to a function called "given"; however, the **given** function acts like a **switch** statement:

```
#!perl
#5_given.pl

use feature "switch";  #Provides access to the given statement

print "Please enter 'yes' or 'no': ";
$response=<STDIN>;
chomp $response;

given ($response) {
        when ("yes") {print "You agree!\n"; }
        when ("no")  {print "Bummer, you don't agree\n"; }
        default     {print "Maybe next time\n"; }
}
```

Note   Depending on the version of Perl that you are using, you may receive the following messages:

given is experimental at 5_given.pl line 10.

when is experimental at 5_given.pl line 11.

when is experimental at 5_given.pl line 12.

This is normal output as these features may change in the future.

 TRY IT!

Only if you are using Perl 5.10 or higher, execute the following command to see a demonstration of the given statement:

```
perl 5_given.pl
```

The while Statement

The **while** loop will continue to execute its statement(s) as long as the condition holds *true*. The syntax of while loops is

```
while (condition) {
    statement(s)
}
```

The following program code is an example of how to verify user input. We want the user to enter a number that is greater than 100, so we will loop via the **while** statement until the user enters the correct number:

```
#!perl
#5_while1.pl
#Verify number entered is greater than 100

print "Please enter a number greater than 100:";
$number=<STDIN>;
```

```perl
while ($number <= 100) {
    print "That is not greater than 100\n";
    print "Please enter a number greater than 100: ";
    $number=<STDIN>;
}

print "Thanks, $number is greater than 100\n";
```

The until Statement

The **until** loop is the logical opposite of the **while** loop. It will continue to execute its statement(s) as long as the condition holds *false*. The syntax of **until** loops is

```perl
until (condition) {
    statement(s)
}
```

The following program code performs the same function as the previous **while** example:

```perl
#!perl
# 5_until.pl
# Verify number entered is greater than 100

print "Please enter a number greater than 100: ";
$number=<STDIN>;

until ($number > 100) {
    print "That is not greater than 100\n";
    print "Please enter a number greater than 100: ";
    $number=<STDIN>;
}

print "Thanks, $number is greater than 100\n";
```

The do Statement

The preceding examples could have been made a little more efficient with a **do** statement. The idea behind a **do** statement is to execute the statements first and then perform the conditional check:

```perl
#!perl
#5_do.pl
#Verify number entered is greater than 100

do  {
   print "Please enter a number greater than 100: ";
   $number=<STDIN>;
} while ($number <= 100);

print "Thanks, $number is greater than 100\n";
```

Either **while** or **until** can be used with a **do** statement to perform the conditional check.

Important Note   The **do** statement is not a loop, even though it may act like one. The loop control statement, like **next** and **last** (covered later in this chapter), cannot be used with a **do** statement.

Alternative to a do Statement

In most cases, a **do** statement isn't necessary. Consider the first example of a **while** loop that was shown previously:

```perl
#!perl
#5_while1.pl
#Verify number entered is greater than 100

print "Please enter a number greater than 100:";
$number=<STDIN>;

while ($number <= 100) {
   print "That is not greater than 100\n";
```

```perl
    print "Please enter a number greater than 100: ";
    $number=<STDIN>;
}

print "Thanks, $number is greater than 100\n";
```

In this example, the first two statements were used to get an initial value for the $number variable. The statements were repeated within the **while** loop to get a new value for $number.

Alternative to a do Statement—Continued

However, we could have also done the following:

```perl
#!perl
#5_while2.pl
#Verify number entered is greater than 100

while ($number <= 100) {
    print "Please enter a number greater than 100: ";
    $number=<STDIN>;
}
```

Consider what happens the first time the condition is checked. The variable $number hasn't been assigned a value, so in a numeric comparison operation, its return value is 0. This value is less than 100; therefore, the condition is true and the user is asked to enter a number. We could have also assigned $number an initial value that would result in the condition being true as well.

Using this sort of **while** loop has an advantage over a **do** statement. While the **do** statement appears to be a loop, it really isn't a loop structure. Looping control that will be covered in the following sections (the **next** and **last** statements) will not work on **do** statements, but will work in **while** loops.

Loop Control: last

You can use the **last** statement to immediately exit from a loop. The following example will have the user enter exam scores and exit out of the **while** loop if the user enters a score of –1:

```perl
#!perl
#5_last1.pl

while (true) {
    print "Please enter a grade(enter -1 to finish): ";
    chomp($score=<STDIN>);
    if ($score == -1) {
        last;
    }
    push(@grades, $score);
}

print "finished\n";
print "@grades";
print "\n";
```

Note:

- While "true" is true in Perl, it isn't true because of any special Perl feature. In the next chapter, we will talk more about what is true and what is false in Perl.

 TRY IT!

Execute the following command to see a demonstration of the last statement:

```
perl 5_last1.pl
```

Breaking Out of Nested Loops

Suppose you want to be able to break out of a loop that is not the loop that you are directly in. For example, you want to break out of a **foreach** loop from a **while** loop that is within the **foreach** loop.

In order to be able to do this, you want to use a label. A label allows you to "mark" a line in your code. If you specify a label when you use the **last** statement, the **last** statement will apply to the loop on the line of the label.

See the following example to see this in practice.

```perl
#!perl
#5_last2.pl
#Example of breaking out of nested loops

@classes=qw(math science history);

#Create a label:
JUMP: foreach $subject (@classes) {
    print "Enter grades for $subject (-2 to finish)\n";

    while (true) {
        print "Please enter a grade(enter -1 to finish): ";
        chomp($score=<STDIN>);
        if ($score == -1) {
            last;  #last to while loop
        }
        if ($score == -2) {
            last JUMP;  #last to the label's loop
        }
    push(@grades, "$subject:$score");
    }
}

foreach $i (@grades) {
    print "$i\n";
}
```

Loop Control: next

The **next** statement is used to execute the next iteration of the loop. The following example will "ignore" any input that is "less than 0" (with the exception of -1):

```perl
#!perl
#5_next.pl

while (true) {
    print "Please enter a grade (enter -1 to finish): ";
    chomp($score=<STDIN>);
    if ($score == -1) {
        last;
    }
    if ($score < 0) {
        print "Bad input, try again\n";
        next;
    }
    push(@grades, $score);
}

print "finished\n";
print "@grades";
print "\n";
```

Additional Resources

In each chapter, resources are provided to provide the learner with a source for more information. These resources may include downloadable source code or links to other books or articles that will provide you more information about the topic at hand.

Resources for this chapter can be found here:

```
https://github.com/Apress/beginning-perl-programming
```

Lab Exercises

Important Note   If you did not finish the previous lab, either finish it before starting this lab or use the completed cb3.pl provided in the lab answers folder.

Edit the file called cb3.pl and perform the following enhancements (save the changes into a file called cb5.pl):

- Create an "if-elsif" statement to handle the value of the user's input for the menu choice. At this point, just have each condition print the value of the variable $choice.

- Create the code for options 1-3 (enter a deposit, withdrawal, and check). Remember, each transaction will be stored as an element in the array @book. The user will provide fields 2-4 (date of transaction, comment, amount of transaction) for deposits and withdrawals. The first field will be DEP for deposits and WD for withdrawals. For checks, the user will provide the check number and that number will be the first field. Examples:

  DEP:12/12/1999:Paycheck:1000

  WD:12/12/1999:ATM withdrawal:80

  101:12/12/1999:Vons:124.89

- Put the menu into loop so the user can continue using the program until option 7 is chosen.

- Create the code of option 7 (exit program).

  Note: Don't worry about error checking at this time.

When you have completed your work, compare your script against the cb5.pl file provided in lab answers.

CHAPTER 6

Conditional Expressions

Numeric Comparison

The following operators can be used to compare numbers:

Operator	Meaning
==	Returns "true" if two numbers are equal to each other
!=	Returns "true" if two numbers are not equal to each other
>	Returns "true" if the first number is greater than the second number
<	Returns "true" if the first number is less than the second number
>=	Returns "true" if the first number is greater or equal to the second number
<=	Returns "true" if the first number is less than or equal to the second number

Examples:

```
DB<1> $num1=100
DB<2> $num2=99
DB<3> if ($num1 == $num2) {print "yes";}
DB<4> if ($num1 <= $num2) {print "yes";}
DB<5> if ($num1 > $num2) {print "yes";}
yes
```

87

© William "Bo" Rothwell of One Course Source, Inc. 2019
W. "Bo" Rothwell, *Beginning Perl Programming*, https://doi.org/10.1007/978-1-4842-5055-6_6

String Comparison

The following operators can be used to compare strings:

Operator	Meaning
eq	Returns true if the strings are exactly the same
ne	Returns true if the strings are not equal to each other
gt	Returns true if the left string is greater than the right string
lt	Returns true if the left string is less than the right string
ge	Returns true if the left string is greater or than equal the right string
le	Returns true if the left string is less than or to equal the right string

Examples:

```
DB<1> $name1="Bob"
DB<2> $name2="Ted"
DB<3> if ($name1 eq $name2) {print "yes";}
DB<4> if ($name1 gt $name2) {print "yes";}
DB<5> if ($name1 lt $name2) {print "yes";}
yes
```

How Can One String Be Greater Than or Less Than Another String?

When the **gt**, **lt**, **ge,** and **le** operators are used to compare strings, they make use of the order of characters provided by the ASCII text table. The first character of each string is compared to see if one is greater than the other:

```
if ("Bob" gt "Ted") {print "yes";}
```

In this case, the outcome is "false" because "B" appears before "T" in the ASCII text table. If the first character of each string is equal, then the next character of each string is used:

```
if ("Bob" gt "Bill") {print "yes";}
```

In this case, the outcome is "true" because "o" appears after "i" in the ASCII text table.

Difference Between String and Numeric Comparison

Numeric comparisons are different than string comparison. For example, the following is "true":

```
DB<1> $var="3.000"
DB<2> if ($var == 3) {print "yes";}
yes
```

While the following isn't true:

```
DB<1> $var="3.000"
DB<2> if ($var eq 3) {print "yes";}
```

This is because, numerically, 3 is the same as 3.000. Since string comparison compares each character of the strings, 3 is not the same as the 3.000 value.

The following shows another example of the difference between numeric comparison and string comparison:

```
DB<1> print "Please enter your choice"
Please enter your choice
DB<2> $choice=<STDIN>
4

DB<3> if ($choice == 4) {print "yes";}
yes
DB<4> if ($choice eq 4) {print "yes";}
```

In this case the numeric comparison returns true because of how Perl converts strings ("4\n" in this case) into numbers when numeric comparison take place.

TRY IT!

Execute the following command to enter the Perl debugger:

```
perl -d -e "1;"
```

Execute the following commands in the Perl debugger to practice using numeric and string comparison operations:

```
$name="Bob";
$age=55;
if ($name eq "Bob") {print "yes";}
if ($age <= 65) {print "yes";}
if ($name lt "Ted") {print "yes";}
if ($name = 15) {print "yes";}
print $name
```

What happened in the last two lines? By using a single equal sign, you performed an assignment operation, not a comparison operation. The $name variable was set to the value of 15 and the statement ($name = 15) returned "true" because the rvalue (right value) of an assignment operation is the return value. 15 is true in Perl.

Exit the Perl debugger by executing the following debugger command:

```
q
```

Pattern Matching

Pattern matching is the process of finding "text patterns" within a string (or, more likely, a variable that contains a string). While pattern matching is covered in detail in a later chapter, the basics are covered here to illustrate how pattern matching can be used in conditional statements.

To search for a pattern in a variable, use the following syntax:

```
if ($str =~ m/pattern/)
```

If the *pattern* exists in the *$str* variable, then "true" is returned.
If the *pattern* doesn't exist in the *$str* variable, then "false" is returned.

For example, the following will print "correct" if the word "good" appears in the variable $stock:

```
$stock="This is a good time to buy stock";
if ($stock =~ m/good/) {
    print "correct\n";
}
```

Using the Outcome of a Statement

You can use the "outcome" of some Perl statements in a conditional evaluation. For example, the following code will use the outcome of the **defined** function:

```
if (defined ($total)) {
    print "The value is: ", $total +8, "\n";
}
else
{
    print 'The variable $total is not defined', "\n";
}
```

Important Note   Not all Perl statements return "true" or "false." Remember, false is a value of either 0 or "", while true is all other values. Some statements (such as **chop**) return a value that isn't meant to be used in a conditional evaluation because it doesn't necessary return true or false:

```
$var="1002";
if (chop $var) { #"true" in this case since chop returns what
was chopped(2)
    print "chopped it\n";
}
if (chop $var) {    #"false" in this case since chop returns
what was chopped(0)
    print "chopped it again\n";
}
```

If you know what a statement returns, you can use this information to determine if the statement succeeds or fails. For example, if the **chop** statement succeeds, it returns a single character. If it fails, the **chop** statement returns a null string. So, by checking the length of the return value, we can determine if the statement succeeds or fails:

```
$var="1002";
if (length (chop $var)) {
    #statements if chop succeeds
} else {
    #statements if chop fails
}
```

File Test Conditions

File testing is the process of determining the "status" of a file. The most common file tests are listed here.

File test	Meaning
-r	Returns "true" if the file is readable by the user who is running the Perl script
-w	Returns "true" if the file is writeable by the user
-x	Returns "true" if the file is executable by the user
-o	Returns "true" if the file is owned by the user
-e	Returns "true" if the file exists
-z	Returns "true" if the file exists and is empty
-s	Returns the size of the file (0 if the file is empty or doesn't exist)
-f	Returns "true" if the file is a "plain file"
-d	Returns "true" if the file is a directory
-T	Returns "true" if the file contains text data
-B	Returns "true" if the file contains binary data

Notes:

- There are more (not commonly used) file test operators; see the Perl documentation (`https://perldoc.perl.org/functions/-X.html`) for the complete list.

The following will prompt the user to input a name of a file and check to see if it is a directory:

```perl
#!perl
#6_dir.pl

print "Please enter the name of a file or directory: ";
$name=<STDIN>;
chomp $name;
if (-d $name) {
    print "$name is a directory\n";
} else {
    print "$name is not a directory\n";
}
```

Notes Regarding Filenames

Very important: Be certain to include quotes around the filename. This isn't just for file testing operations, but whenever you specify a filename in Perl. Exception: When using a variable that contains a filename, quotes are not needed.

Another concern regarding filenames is related to how different operating systems handle directory separators. For example, on Linux and Unix systems, the following path is valid:

```
/usr/share/dict/linux.words
```

While on Window systems, the following path is valid:

```
\temp\file.txt
```

Unfortunately, the "\" character has a special meaning in Perl (recall "\n" represents a newline character and "\t" represents a tab character). This means if you use the Windows directory separator character, you need to place the path in single quotes:

```
'\temp\file.txt'
```

However, you never had to use "\" when specifying pathnames. Perl is smart enough to use the right separator, so you can always use "/" even if you are working on a Windows system.

 TRY IT!

Execute the following command to enter the Perl debugger:

```
perl -d -e "1;"
```

Execute the following commands in the Perl debugger to practice using file test operations:

```
if (-f "6_dir.pl") {print "yes";};
if (-T "6_dir.pl") {print "yes";};
if (-d "6_dir.pl") {print "yes";};
print "The files 6_dir.pl is ", -s "6_dir.pl", " bytes large";
```

Exit the Perl debugger by executing the following debugger command:

```
q
```

Complex Conditional Expressions

Suppose you wish to set up an automatic grading program, which will assign a student a letter grade based upon a numeric score (91-100 = "A", 81-90 = "B"). In this case, you would want to check the students' grade to see if it is between two scores. Complex conditional expressions allow you to do this.

Logical and

To find if two (or more) conditional statements, use the "&&" operator:

```
if (($score <= 100) && ($score >90)) {
   print "Your score is an 'A'\n";
}
```

Logical or

To find if one of several conditional statements is true, use the "||" operator:

```
if (($age > 55) || ($age < 16)) {
   print "Eligible for discount\n";
}
```

Logical not

To reverse the outcome of a conditional statement, use the "!" operator:

```
if (! (-r $file)) {
print "Sorry, you can't read $file\n ";
}
```

Notes:

- The "!" operator will reverse the outcome of an expression, making a "false" outcome "true" and a "true" outcome "false."

- For program readability, use the logical **not** where it is, well…logical. For example, the conditional statement (!($num < 25)) is the same as ($num >= 25). The second statement is easier to read.

 TRY IT!

Execute the following command to enter the Perl debugger:

```
perl -d -e "1;"
```

Execute the following commands in the Perl debugger to practice complex conditional expressions:

```
$name="Bob";
$age=25;
if ($name eq "Bob" && $age == 25) {print "yes";};
if ($name eq "Ted" || $age == 25) {print "yes";};
```

```
if (! -d "6_dir.pl") {print "6_dir.pl is not a directory";};
```

Exit the Perl debugger by executing the following debugger command:

```
q
```

Understand and/or vs. &&/||

You may see the operators **or** and **and** used in place of || and **&&**. There is a subtle, but sometimes important, difference between **or** vs. || (as well as **and** vs. **&&)**. In many cases they will produce the same results; however, **or** and **and** have a lower precedence than || and **&&.**

Consider the following code:

```
DB<1> $test="abc"
DB<2> $new = $junk or $test
DB<3> print $new
```

The intent was to assign $new to $junk IF the $junk variable was defined. If it was not defined, then we wanted $new to be assigned to $test. However, since **or** has a lower precedence than the assignment operation, the way this statement really executed was as follows:

```
DB<2> ($new = $junk) or $test
```

The correct way to handle this would be to use ||:

```
DB<4> $new = $junk || $test
DB<5> print $new
abc
```

Understand and/or vs. &&/||—Continued

Consider the following code:

```
DB<1> @info=stat("sub1.pl") || die
DB<2> print "@info"
1
```

Our intention was to run the **stat** function, and if it failed to return the data needed from the "sub1.pl" file, use the **die** statement to exit the program. Unfortunately, we end up with the wrong data stored in @info if the **stat** function succeeds.

Because of precedence, what is really happening here is this:

```
DB<1> @info= (stat("sub1.pl") || die)
```

If the **stat** function is successful, then the resulting "rvalue" is 1 for "true" because one of the two statements returned true, making the entire statement true. If you use **or** instead of ||, you will get the correct results:

```
DB<3> @info=stat("sub1.pl") or die
DB<4> print "@info"
2 0 33206 1 0 0 2 119 1355943060 1355943094 1355943060
```

Using Parentheses

You can override the default precedence of conditional operators by using parentheses. Consider the following example:

```
DB<1> $name="Bob"
DB<2> $age=25
DB<3> $title="manager"
DB<4> if ($name eq "Nick" && $age == 40 || $title eq "manager") {print "yes";}
yes
DB<5> if ($name eq "Nick" && ($age == 40 || $title eq "manager")) {print "yes";}
```

The conditional expression on line #4 returns "true" if

$name equals "Nick" AND $age equals 40

or

$title equals manager

The conditional expression on line #5 returns "true" if

$name equals "Nick"

and

$age equals 40 OR $title equals manager

Short Circuiting

Perl permits an alternative to the **if** statement called "short circuiting." This method uses either the "logical and" or the "logical or" operators. Consider the following code:

```perl
if ($x < 16) {
    print "Too young to drive\n";
}
```

This code could be written using this syntax:

```perl
($x < 16) && print "Too young to drive\n";
```

This method is made possible due to the following:

1. Logical operators are not only allowed within conditional statements (they can exist just about anywhere in a Perl script).

2. If the first part of a "logical and" statement isn't "true," Perl won't execute the second part (because the entire statement can't be true).

 TRY IT!

Execute the following command to enter the Perl debugger:

```
perl -d -e "1;"
```

Execute the following commands in the Perl debugger to practice different "if-like" conditional statements:

```perl
$name="Ted";
if ($name eq "Ted") {print "yes";};
print "yes" if $name eq "Ted";
$name eq "Ted" && print "yes";
```

Exit the Perl debugger by executing the following debugger command:

```
q
```

Additional Resources

In each chapter, resources are provided to provide the learner with a source for more information. These resources may include downloadable source code or links to other books or articles that will provide you more information about the topic at hand.

Resources for this chapter can be found here:

```
https://github.com/Apress/beginning-perl-programming
```

Lab Exercises

Important Note   If you did not finish the previous lab, either finish it before starting this lab or use the completed cb5.pl provided in the lab answers folder.

Edit the file called cb5.pl and perform the following enhancements (save the changes into a file called cb6.pl):

- Perform the following error checking:

    1.   Check the value of $name (make sure it's not empty).

    2.   Check the value of $choice (should be either 1, 2, 3, 4, 5, 6, or 7).

    3.   For options 1-3, check the user's input for the amount of the transaction (should be a number that is greater than 0).

When you have completed your work, compare your script against the cb6.pl file provided in lab answers.

CHAPTER 7

Basic Input and Output

Reading Input

There are several methods of reading input that will be discussed in the next two chapters:

- The standard input filehandle

- The diamond operator

- User-created filehandles (discussed in a later chapter)

The most common method of reading input is the *standard input filehandle*. A filehandle is a connection between your script and a "port." The standard input filehandle reads data from the port connected to standard input (data coming from the keyboard by default).

The user who runs the program can "redirect" the origin of standard input to come from a file or the output of a command rather than from the keyboard by using one of the following syntaxes:

```
[student@ocs student]$ script.pl < file   #standard input comes from the
"file"
[student@ocs student]$ cmd | script.pl  # standard input comes from the
output of the "cmd"
```

<STDIN> represents the standard input filehandle:

```
print "Please enter your age:";
$age=<STDIN>;
```

101

© William "Bo" Rothwell of One Course Source, Inc. 2019
W. "Bo" Rothwell, *Beginning Perl Programming*, https://doi.org/10.1007/978-1-4842-5055-6_7

Note   For redirection to work correctly on Win32 systems, you must execute your program as follows:

```
perl script.pl
while & until Loops
```

The **while** and **until** loops are useful for reading in multiple lines of text. For example, the following will read a line of a time from standard input and print out each line with its line number preceding it:

```
#!perl
#7_line.pl

while ($line=<STDIN>) {           #reads a line at a time from standard input
    print "$.  $line";
}
```

Notes:

- The statement **$line=<STDIN>** stores the line read into the variable $line.

- The **while** loop will "fail" when (**$line=<STDIN>**) returns "false." This will happen when either:

  - The end of the file is reached (when a command like "script.pl < file" is executed).

  - The end of the piped command's output is reached ("cmd | script.pl").

  - The user terminates the input with ^D (UNIX/Linux) or ^Z (Win32).

- The special variable **$.** holds the number of the line that is currently being read from the filehandle.

✂ **Cool Trick**   You can read STDIN into an array using the following syntax:

```
@arr=<STDIN>;
```

 **TRY IT!**

Execute the following command to test reading data via loops:

```
perl 7_line.pl
```

When prompted for input, enter the following three lines and note the output that is produced:

```
Line 1
Second line
Last line
```

After entering all these three lines, terminate the input by using one of the two methods:

On Windows-based machines: Control+z, then hit the <Enter> key

On Linux and Unix machines: Control+d

Record Separator Variable

The "record separator variable" stores the character(s) that Perl uses to "break up" the data that is read from the filehandle. In other words, it contains the delimiter character for input.

The record separator variable name is **$/**. By default, it is set to the newline character ("\n") and, in almost every case, should not be changed. However, there are a couple of situations in which changing this variable can make life a little easier.

Reading Flat Databases

Suppose we had a database file which contained a completely flat database:

Ted:9930:accounting:Bob:9940:HR:Sue:9950:accounting:

In this case, we could change the **$/** variable to a colon (":") and read the entire file into an array with each element being a field in the array:

```
$/=":";
@fields=<STDIN>;
chomp (@fields);
$/="\n";
```

Notes:

- The **chomp** command actually chomps whatever the **$/** variable is set to.

- It's important to set the **$/** variable back to a newline character as soon as you are finished reading the file.

Read an Entire File into a Scalar Variable

When you read a file into a scalar variable, since the **$/** variable is set to a newline character, only the first line is read into the variable:

```
$line=<STDIN>;
```

You can read an entire file into a variable, but by default it has to be an array variable:

```
@file=<STDIN>;
```

If you undefined the record separator variable, then Perl "doesn't know when to stop" reading from a file. So, it reads the entire file into the scalar variable:

```
undef $/;
$line=<STDIN>;        #reads entire standard input into $line
$/="\n";
```

The Diamond Operator

The <STDIN> operator can read data from standard input. Standard input can come from any of the following:

The keyboard:

```
[student@ocs student]$ ./script.pl
reads data from keyboard
```

Redirected from a file:

```
[student@ocs student]$ ./script.pl < file1
```

Redirected from another command:

[student@ocs student]$ **cmd | ./script.pl**

However, the <STDIN> operator can't read files that are given as arguments:

[student@ocs student]$ **./script.pl file1.txt file2.txt file3.txt**

In the proceeding example, if the <STDIN> operator is used, the data will be gathered from the keyboard.

Note:

- Remember to include "perl" before the script name in the Win32 environment.

The <> (diamond) operator can read data just like <STDIN> (from standard input), but it can also read data from files listed as command line arguments.

```perl
#!perl
#7_count.pl
# This program will count the number of lines that contain the word "echo"

$total=0;    #not required, just good style

while ($line=<>) {
   if ($line =~ /echo/) {
      $total++;
   }
}
print "Number of lines that contain 'echo': $total\n";
```

Note:

- The @ARGV variables (which contains the command line arguments) is "emptied" as a result of reading from the <> operator.

- The statement **$line** =~ /**echo**/ is a regular expression pattern matching that will return "true" if "echo" appears in the variable $line.

Warning: Problem with Redirection

Redirection poses a couple of problems for a programmer. Consider the following example:

```
[student@ocs student]$ ./script.pl < example.txt
```

In this example, the operating system (OS) opens the file, example.txt, and sends it into the Perl script as the script requests it. In other words, it's the OS, not the Perl script, that "gets the data."

This action presents two problems for the programmer:

1. Since the programmer is just handed "data," the programmer can't perform file test operators on the file. In addition, the file can't be reopened by the programmer later in the script. The programmer doesn't know anything about where the data comes from, which greatly limits the programmer.

2. Once a user implements redirection, the OS will ALWAYS send standard input from the redirected location. This effectively prevents the programmer from receiving data from the user because <STDIN> tries to read from the redirected file (or command).

Using the diamond operator to read data from files listed as command line arguments can eliminate this problem. Using this technique, you can use <STDIN> to read data from the keyboard. In addition, you can only redirect one file, but the <> operator will read from all of the files listed on the command line.

The Default Variable

The default variable is useful in situations like the last script. Instead of assigning <STDIN> or <> to a variable, we can just specify the operator:

```
while (<STDIN>)
```

The data is stored in the special variable $_. Using this method allows you to perform some shortcuts in your Perl script:

1. You don't have to create a new variable (a little less typing).

2. Many Perl statements (**chomp**, **chop**, **print**, regular expression pattern matching, etc.) will assume you want to operate on the default variable unless you specify something else.

For example, the last script could be changed to look like this:

```perl
#!perl
#7_echo.pl
# This program will count the number of lines that contain the word "echo"

$total=0;   #not required, just good style

while (<>) {
   if (/echo/) {           #Assumes to look in $_ for "echo"
      $total++;
   }
}
print "Number of lines that contain 'echo': $total\n";
```

TRY IT!

Execute the following command to enter the Perl debugger:

```
perl -d -e "1;"
```

Execute the following commands in the Perl debugger to practice using the default variable:

```perl
$_="hello there\n";
print;
chomp;
print;
if (m/hello/) {print "yes";};
chop; chop; chop;
print;
```

Exit the Perl debugger by executing the following debugger command:

```
q
```

Using Parentheses

The **print** statement is pretty straightforward...as long as you don't do this:

```
print (5+6)*8, " is the result";
```

In this case we are trying to print a mathematical operation, (5+6)∗8, followed by a string. The result of this **print** statement isn't what we expected:

```
11
```

Why 11? To understand this, you need to understand how parentheses are used in Perl. Parentheses have many different meanings in Perl. For example, they are used to create lists and to specify grouping in regular expressions.

In addition to specifying precedence in mathematical expressions, parentheses are also used to specify the parameters that you want to pass into a statement:

```
print ("This is the formal way to type a print statement!");
```

When Perl sees **print (5+6)∗8** it thinks that the result of 5+6 (11) is a parameter to be passed into the **print** statement. To avoid this, just make your **print** statement a little more formal:

```
print ((5+6)*8, " is the result");
```

Additional Resources

In each chapter, resources are provided to provide the learner with a source for more information. These resources may include downloadable source code or links to other books or articles that will provide you more information about the topic at hand.

Resources for this chapter can be found here:

```
https://github.com/Apress/beginning-perl-programming
```

Lab Exercises

There won't be any need to use the topics that were learned in this chapter in the checkbook program that you have been creating, so this lab exercise will be for a standalone program. For this lab, create a program that will read a sentence from a user one line at a time.

The user should be prompted for a sentence and informed to press <ENTER> when they have completed the sentence. To end the input, the user should type either Control-d (for Linux or Unix systems) or Control-z + <ENTER> (for Windows systems).

Take the user input and place it all into a single scalar variable (forming a paragraph). After all input has been received, print the user's new paragraph on the screen. Hint: You probably want to put some spaces between those sentences!

When you have completed your work, compare your script against the paragraph.pl file provided in lab answers.

CHAPTER 8

Advanced Input and Output

Filehandles

A filehandle is a connection between your script and a "port." There are four standard filehandles in Perl by default:

<STDIN>	Standard input
<>	Standard input or files listed on command line
STDOUT	Standard output
STDERR	Standard error

The <STDIN> and <> filehandles were covered in a previous chapter. The STDOUT filehandle is the port used to send messages to the screen. When you use the **print** statement, it sends the output to the STDOUT filehandle by default.

The STDERR filehandle will be discussed in the "The die and warn Functions" section.

You can also create your own filehandles that can be used to read from files, write to files, and pipe data to or from OS commands.

The die and warn Functions

The **die** function will print an error message and exit from your script:

```perl
if (!(-r $filename)) {
    die "Could not read from file $filename\n";
}
```

© William "Bo" Rothwell of One Course Source, Inc. 2019
W. "Bo" Rothwell, *Beginning Perl Programming*, https://doi.org/10.1007/978-1-4842-5055-6_8

Notes:

- The output of **die** will go to the standard error port, STDERR. This will normally be set to the screen but can be redirected by the user who is running the script.

- If a newline character (\n) appears at the end of the die message, just the message is printed on the screen.

- If there isn't a newline character at the end of the die message, the message and the line in the script that the **die** statement appeared on is printed on the screen.

- By itself (with no message), **die** will print "Died" followed by the line number at which the script died.

die example

```perl
#!perl
#8_die.pl

if (!(-r "/etc/junkfile")) {
    die "can't find file"
}

print "go on from here with more code";
```

Output of 8_die.pl

```
[student@ocs student]$ ./8_die.pl
can't find file at ./8_die.pl line 5.
```

Returning an Exit Status Value with die

All OS commands provide an exit status value when they finish executing. An exit value of 0 means the command completed successfully. An exit value between 1 and 255 means the command failed.

Exit values are useful to the person who executed the command, as different values can indicate why the command failed. You can have the **die** statement provide an exit value by setting the value to the **$!** variable prior to executing the **die** statement:

```
$!=2;
die "File not found\n";
```

Using the exit Statement

If you don't want to produce an error message to STDOUT, but you want to stop the execution of your program, use the **exit** statement. To specify an exit value, specify a numeric argument to the exit command:

```
exit 1
```

The **warn** statement will print an error message but continue executing the code in your script:

```
if (!(-r $filename)) {
    warn "Could not read from $filename\n";
}
```

The preceding notes about the **die** statement also apply to the **warn** statement. Warn example:

```
#!perl
#8_warn.pl

if (!(-r "/etc/junkfile")) {warn "can't find file"};
if (!(-r "/etc/junkfile")) {warn "can't find file\n"};
if (!(-r "/etc/junkfile")) {print STDERR "can't find file\n"};
```

Output of 8_warn.pl

```
[student@ocs student]$ ./8_warn.pl
can't find file at ./8_warn.pl line 4.
can't find file
can't find file
```

Opening and Reading from Files

To open a file to read from, use the **open** statement:

```
open (HANDLE, "<file_to_open") || die "could not open file";
```

Notes:

- The "<" symbol tells Perl to open the file for reading. This symbol is often omitted as Perl assumes the file is being opened for reading.

- Filenames must always be presented in string format (i.e., you need to put quotes around the filename).

Once a file has been opened, you can read from it by using the filehandle like <STDIN>. For example, to read a line from the file into the variable $line, execute the following:

```
$line=<HANDLE>;
```

Use the **close** statement to close the filehandle:

```
close HANDLE;
```

Different Ways of Opening Files

As of Perl 5.6, you can use a feature called "indirect filehandles." This technique allows you to store a filehandle into a variable instead of using a "hard-coded" filehandle name:

```
open ($read_file, "<file_to_open") || die "could not open file";
```

To access the data from the file, just use the variable in place of the previously used filehandle name:

```
$line=<$read_file>;
```

As of Perl 5.6, you can use either the two argument technique or three argument technique to the **open** statement:

```
open ($FILE, "<junk.txt") || die;
open ($FILE, "<", "junk.txt") || die;
```

With the three argument technique, the second argument is how you want to open the file. By making this a separate argument, it is clearer to read and avoid the following rare potential error:

```
$file=">abc.txt";          #Filename is really called ">abc.txt"
open $file, ">$file";      #will append to a file called "abc.txt",
                           #not overwrite it as  planned
```

TRY IT!

Execute the following command to enter the Perl debugger:

```
perl -d -e "1;"
```

Execute the following commands in the Perl debugger to practice opening and reading from filehandles:

```
open ($input, "<", "8_warn.pl") || die;
$line=<$input>;
print $line;
close $input;
```

Exit the Perl debugger by executing the following debugger command:

```
q
```

Opening and Writing to Files

To open a file to write to, use the **open** statement:

```
open (HANDLE, ">file_to_open") || die "could not open file";
```

Notes:

- The ">" symbol tells Perl to open the file for writing. If the file already exists, then Perl will overwrite the file contents.

- To append to the end of the file, use the append symbol: ">>".

Once a file has been opened, you can write to it by using the **print** statement and specifying the filehandle to print to:

```
print HANDLE "First line of text\n";
print HANDLE "Second line of text\n";
```

The process of closing the filehandle will close the port and write all of the output to the file:

```
close HANDLE;
```

TRY IT!

Execute the following command to enter the Perl debugger:

```
perl -d -e "1;"
```

Execute the following commands in the Perl debugger to practice opening and writing from filehandles:

```
open ($output, ">", "data.txt") || die;
print $output "First line of output\n";
print $output "Second line\n";
close $output;
```

Exit the Perl debugger by executing the following debugger command:

```
q
```

View the new file that you created by executing the following command:

```
more data.txt
```

Reading a Block of a Filehandle

The **read** statement can be used to read a block of a filehandle. The syntax is

```
read (FILEHANDLE, $var_to_store_read, #_of_bytes_to_read);
```

For example, to read 6 characters in a filehandle:

```
read (STDIN, $input, 6);
```

Notes:

- The filehandle can't be in brackets (STDIN, not <STDIN>).

- Perl keeps track of how far into the file you have read. So, another **read** statement would read from character 7 in the aforementioned example.

TRY IT!

Execute the following command to enter the Perl debugger:

```
perl -d -e "1;"
```

Execute the following commands in the Perl debugger to practice opening and reading from filehandles with the read statement:

```
open ($input, "<", "8_warn.pl") || die;
read ($input, $data, 10);
print $data;
close $input;
```

Exit the Perl debugger by executing the following debugger command:

```
q
```

Reading a Single Character

The **getc** statement reads just one character from a filehandle. The syntax for the **getc** statement is

```
$var = getc FILEHANDLE;
```

In the following example, a filehandle is opened and the first three characters are read:

```
open (DATA, "/tmp/data");
$first = getc DATA;
$second = getc DATA;
$third = getc DATA;
close DATA;
```

Notes:

- The filehandle can't be in brackets (DATA, not <DATA>).

- Perl keeps track of how far into the file you have read. So, if you didn't close the filehandle, another **getc** statement would read from character 4 in the aforementioned example.

Piping in Perl

You can open filehandles that take the output of an OS command and sends it into your Perl script. Once again, the **open** statement creates the filehandle:

```
open (HANDLE, "ps -fe |");
```

Note   The command "ps -fe" will run the UNIX command that lists the processes that are running on the system. The "|" symbol after the "ps -fe" command tells Perl to run the "ps -fe" command and then send this data into the filehandle.

Once the **open** statement has been executed, you can read from it by using the filehandle like <STDIN>. For example, to read a line from the output of the command into the variable $line, execute the following:

```
$line=<HANDLE>;
```

The process of closing the filehandle will close the port:

```
close HANDLE;
```

Sending Data to an OS Command

Not only can you read the output of OS commands sent into your script, you can also send output from your script into an OS command. For example, suppose you had a large amount of text to display on the screen (more than a screen's worth). You want the user to have the features of the "more" command to control the display of the text:

```
open (HANDLE, "| more");
```

The "|" symbol before the "more" command tells Perl to send the output of the filehandle HANDLE to the "more" command.

Once the **open** statement has been executed, you can write to it by using the filehandle just like STDOUT. For example, to write the entire contents of an array to the filehandle:

```
print HANDLE "@array";
```

> **Note**   The "more" command isn't executed until the filehandle is closed. The
> process of closing the filehandle will close the port and send the data to the OS
> command:
>
> ```
> close HANDLE;
> ```

Example of sending data to an OS command

```perl
#!perl
#8_more.pl

open (MORE, "| more") || die "can't do this";

for ($i=1;$i < 100 ; $i++) {
   print MORE "$i\n";
   }

close MORE
```

 TRY IT!

Execute the following command to see a demonstration of writing data to an OS command:

```
perl 8_more.pl
```

The format Statement

Perl provides a method of creating formatted output with the **format** and **write**
statements. The **format** statement is used to create a template, while the **write** statement
is used to send the output to a filehandle.

To create a template, use the following syntax:

```
format FILEHANDLE =
Plain text and placeholder: @>>>>>
$var    #variable values go in placeholder
.
```

Notes:

- The value of the variable will go in the "placeholder," @>>>>> in the preceding example.

- The FILEHANDLE can be STDOUT, STDERR, or a filehandle that you create with an **open** statement.

- Each filehandle can only have one **format** statement because the template is created at compile time, not run time.

- The . (dot) must be on a line by itself. This character indicates the end of the **format** statement.

After the variables have been set and the filehandle has been opened, use the **write** statement to send the output to the filehandle:

```
write FILEHANDLE;
```

Basic Placeholders

There are many different types of placeholders that can be used with the **format** statement. These placeholders tell the write command how to place the contents of the variables to the filehandle. The following describes some of the basic placeholders:

Placeholder type	Meaning
@<<<	Left justify the text
@>>>	Right justify the text
@|||	Center the text
@##.##	Numeric output (lines up decimal place)

Notes:

- Each placeholder character represents one character of the variable, so @<<< means "four characters, left justified."

- If there aren't enough placeholder characters to "fit" all of the variable's characters, the extra characters are truncated. For example, if the contents of a variable is the string "abcde" and the placeholder is @<<, then only "abc" would be displayed in the placeholder's "space."

Example of basic placeholders:

```
#!perl
#8_form1.pl

format STDOUT =
@||||||||||||
$title
Name: @<<<<<   Age: @<<
      $name,        $age
code: @>>>>>>>>
$code
Sale #1: @####.##
         $sale1
Sale #2: @####.##
         $sale2
Sale #3: @####.##
         $sale3
.

$title="Status";
$name="bob smith";
$age=25;
$code="674AR3";
$sale1=123;                $sale2=9.99;            $sale3=45.8;

write STDOUT;
```

Output of 8_form1.pl

```
[student@ocs student]$ ./8_form1.pl
   Status
Name: bob sm   Age: 25
code:    674AR3
Sale #1:       123.00
Sale #2:         9.99
Sale #3:        45.80
```

Demonstrating Truncation

To demonstrate that truncation has occurred, use "..." at the end of your field:

```perl
#!perl
#8_form_trunc.pl

format STDOUT =
Name: @<<<<<<<...
      $name
.

$name="Mr. My";

write STDOUT;

$name="Mr. My Name Is Too Long";

write STDOUT;
```

Output of 8_form_trunc.pl

```
[student@ocs student]$ ./8_form_trunc.pl
Name: Mr. My
Name: Mr. My N...
```

Numeric Fields

The following program demonstrates three numeric field features:

1. You can use "^0####" to pad with zeros instead of spaces.

2. When truncating is required for floating point values, rounding up will occur.

3. An "error" will occur when the size of the variable exceeds the allocated field size.

```perl
#!perl
#8_form_num.pl
```

```
format STDOUT =
Sale #1: @O###.##
         $sale1
Sale #2: @####.##
         $sale2
Sale #3: @####.##
         $sale3
.

$sale1=123;
$sale2=9.4587;
$sale3=4444445.8;

write STDOUT;
```

Output of 8_form_num.pl :

```
[student@ocs student]$ ./8_form_num.pl
Sale #1: 00123.00
Sale #2:     9.46
Sale #3: ########
```

Advanced Placeholders

In addition to the basic placeholders, the format statement also supports

Placeholder type	Meaning
^<<<	Left justify, break up over multiple lines if needed
@*	Left justify, multi-line output

Example of Advanced Placeholders

```
#!perl
#8_form_2.pl

format STDOUT =
Comment: @*
$comment
```

```
Keywords: ^<<<<<<
          $keywords
          ^<<<<<<
          $keywords
.

$comment="Displays good tact\nworks hard\nsometimes is late";
$keywords="work effort";

write STDOUT;
```

Output of 8_form2.pl

[student@ocs student]$ **./8_form2.pl**
Comment: Displays good tact
works hard
sometimes is late
Keywords: work
*   effort*

Repeating Lines

As previously shown, the "^" placeholder character will break up text across multiple lines:

```
format STDOUT =
Keywords:^<<<<<<
         $keywords
         ^<<<<<<
         $keywords
.
```

Unfortunately, this method is cumbersome and sometimes will produce undesirable results. For example, the variable $keywords is declared like this:

```
$keywords="work    effort    late    raise";
```

The words "late" and "raise" would never be printed.

To say "repeat this line over and over until the variable is empty," use the ~~ characters at the beginning of the line:

```
format STDOUT =
Keywords:^<<<<<<
         $keywords
~~       ^<<<<<<
         $keywords
```

Note that as of Perl 5.6, the ~~ characters can appear at the end of the line.

Example of repeating lines

```
#!perl
```
#8_form_3.pl

```
format STDOUT =
Keywords: ^<<<<<<
          $keywords
~~        ^<<<<<<
          $keywords
.

$keywords="work effort late raise";

write STDOUT;
```

 TRY IT!

Execute the following command to see a demonstration of repeating lines in format statement:

```
perl 8_form3.pl
```

Here Document

Here documents are useful when you have a "chunk" of data that you want to print and there is no need for fancy formatting. The syntax of the here document is

```
print << "EOF";
These are the lines
of text that will
be printed
EOF
```

All of the text from the first EOF to the second EOF will be sent to the **print** statement. A simple **print** statement with newline characters in the string will work as well:

```
print "These are the lines\nof text that will\nbe printed";
```

However, some programmers don't like this method because it isn't WYSIWYG (What You See Is What You Get). A non-here method that is WYSIWYG is

```
print "
These are the lines
of text that will
be printed";
```

Here example

```
#!perl
#8_here.pl

#Using a here document:
print <<'EOF';
these are the lines of text to send to bob
This service costs $0
EOF

print "\n\n";

#Using a print statement, option #1:
print "\nthese are the lines of text to send to bob\nThis service costs \$0\n";

print "\n\n";
```

```
#Using a print statement, option #2:
print '
these are the lines of text to send to bob
This service costs $0';

print "\n\n";
```

Output of 8_here.pl

```
# ./8_here.pl
these are the lines of text to send to bob
This service costs $0

these are the lines of text to send to bob
This service costs $0

these are the lines of text to send to bob
This service costs $0
```

Additional Resources

In each chapter, resources are provided to provide the learner with a source for more information. These resources may include downloadable source code or links to other books or articles that will provide you more information about the topic at hand.

Resources for this chapter can be found here:

```
https://github.com/Apress/beginning-perl-programming
```

Lab Exercises

Important Note   If you did not finish the previous lab, either finish it before starting this lab or use the completed cb6.pl provided in the lab answers folder.

Edit the file called cb6.pl and perform the following enhancements (save the changes into a file called cb8.pl):

- Change all of the error messages throughout your program to either warn statements or print statements that print to STDERR.

- To have this database script permanently store all of the transactions, we will need to store this data in a file. The name of the file will be the user's name followed by ".data". For example, if the user's name is "ted," then the file will be "ted.data". Change the code in your script so that prior to printing the menu, it checks to see if this file exists. If it does, read each line into your array @book. If it doesn't, create the array @book based on user input.

- When your script exits, have it print all of the elements in the @book array into the database file mentioned in the previous bullet item (name.data). Suggestion: Overwrite the entire contents of the file with the contents of the @book array (don't append).

When you have completed your work, compare your script against the cb8.pl file provided in lab answers.

CHAPTER 9

Pattern Matching

Pattern Matching vs. Wildcards

Operating systems use "wildcards" in order to make referring to filenames easier. The idea of regular expressions (or patterns) in Perl is very much like wildcards...at least conceptually. While wildcards are special characters that refer to filenames, regular expressions are special characters that refer to text within a string.

While most operating systems only have a few wildcards, Perl has many regular expressions (see the "Modifiers" section). In this manual, for brevity, a regular expression is often referred to as "RE."

Matching, Substitution, and Translation

There are three different operators that use regular expressions: the matching, substitution, and translation operators.

The Matching Operator

This operator is most useful in a conditional statement. It returns either a true or false value depending on if the regular expressions we are searching for exist in the scalar variable we specify:

```
if ($var =~ m/error/) {
    print "ERROR\n";
}
```

Note The "m" can be dropped: (/error/).

© William "Bo" Rothwell of One Course Source, Inc. 2019
W. "Bo" Rothwell, *Beginning Perl Programming*, https://doi.org/10.1007/978-1-4842-5055-6_9

The Substitution Operator

This operator is useful for searching for regular expressions within a string and replacing it with another string. For example, the following will replace the string "dog" with "cat" in the variable $var:

```
$var="The dog is outside";
$var =~ s/dog/cat/;
```

The Translation Operator

This operator is useful for translating characters. For example, suppose you want to translate all lowercase characters in a variable to uppercase characters:

```
$var="The dog is outside";
$var =~ tr/abcdefghijklmnopqrstuvwxyz/ABCDEFGHIJKLMNOPQRSTUVWXYZ/;
```

Notes:

- There is a much easier way of doing the preceding example, which will be shown later.

- The translation operation can also be done using the **y** operator: y/abc/xyz/.

- Be careful... the number of characters on each "side" (abc/xyz) should be the same. Perl won't report an error, but the result won't be what you intended.

Throughout the rest of this chapter, the different types of regular expressions are shown using the matching, substitution, and translation operators.

TRY IT!

Execute the following command to enter the Perl debugger:

```
perl -d -e "1;"
```

Execute the following commands in the Perl debugger to practice matching, substitution, and translation operations (recall that the default variable, $_, is used when no variable is specified):

```
$_="Perl is a fun language";
print;
if (m/fun/) {print "yes";};
s/fun/Great/;
print;
tr/PG/pg/;
print;
```

Exit the Perl debugger by executing the following debugger command:

```
q
```

Modifiers

As their name implies, modifiers change how the matching, substitution, and translation operators behave. They are placed at the end of the statement. The most common modifiers are "g" and "i".

The "g" Modifier

When Perl looks for a pattern, it only looks for the first pattern in the string. Once found, it doesn't look for any other pattern matches:

```
$var="The dog is eating out of the dog bowl";
$var =~ s/dog/cat/;

# The result is "The cat is eating out of the dog bowl"
```

To have Perl find all the regular expressions in the string that match, use the "g" (global) modifier:

```
$var="The dog is eating out of the dog bowl";
$var =~ s/dog/cat/g;

# The result is "The cat is eating out of the cat bowl"
```

Note   The translation operator doesn't ever require the "g" modifier since it looks at the entire string by default.

The "i" Modifier

Perl treats uppercase and lowercase letters as different characters (in other words, Perl is a case sensitive environment). To tell Perl to perform a case insensitive search, use the "i" operator:

```
if ($var =~ /abc/i) {
    print "found it!\n";
}
```

Note   The translation operator doesn't accept the "i" modifier.

 TRY IT!

Execute the following command to enter the Perl debugger:

```
perl -d -e "1;"
```

Execute the following commands in the Perl debugger to practice the "i" and "g" modifiers (recall that the default variable, $_, is used when no variable is specified):

```
$_="Perl is a fun language - learn Perl!";
if (m/perl/) {print "yes";};
if (m/perl/i) {print "yes"};
```

```
s/Perl/Linux/;
print;
$_="Perl is a fun language - learn Perl!";
s/Perl/Linux/g;
print;
```

Exit the Perl debugger by executing the following debugger command:

```
q
```

Regular Expressions: Metacharacters

Metacharacters are special characters in a pattern that "represent" other strings. The following characters are the metacharacters in Perl:

Character	Meaning
*	Represents the previous character repeated zero or more times.
+	Represents the previous character repeated one or more times.
{x,y}	Represents the previous character repeated *x* to *y* times.
.	Represents exactly one character (any one character).
[ ]	Represents any single character listed within the bracket. The ^ character in the beginning changes the meaning to represent any single character NOT listed within the brackets.
?	Represents an optional character. The character prior to "?" is optional.
^	Represents the beginning of the line when it is the first character in the RE.
$	Represents the end of the line when it is the last character in the RE.
( )	Used to group an expression.
|	Represents an "or" operator.
\	Used to "escape" the special meaning of the preceding characters.

"∗" Examples

The "∗" character matches "zero or more of the previous character." Some examples are as follows:

```
DB<1> $_="Code: abbbbc"
DB<2> if (/ab*c/) {print "yes";}
yes
DB<3> print
Code: abbbbc
DB<4> s/ab*c/---/
DB<5> print
Code: ---
```

"+" Examples

The "+" character matches "one or more of the previous character." Some examples are as follows:

```
DB<1> $_="Code: abbbbc"
DB<2> if (/ab*c/) {print "yes";}
yes
DB<3> if (/ab+c/) {print "yes";}
yes
DB<4> $_="Code: ac"
DB<5> if (/ab*c/) {print "yes";}
yes
DB<6> if (/ab+c/) {print "yes";}
```

Notice that the conditional statement for line #5 returned true, but the conditional statement for line #6 returned false. This is because "b∗" can literally match nothing at all, while "b+" must match at least one "b" character.

Warning About Using "*"

Because the "*" character can match "zero" characters, you may run into problems when using it:

```
DB<1> $_="Code: abbbbc"
DB<2> if (/x*y*z*/) {print "yes";}
yes
```

The output for line #2 may seem wrong because there are no "x", "y", or "z" characters to match, but that is the point of the "*" character. In line #2 of this example, you are matching "zero or more 'x' characters, followed by zero or more 'y' characters, followed by zero or more 'z' characters." What exactly does this match? See the following:

```
DB<1> $_="Code: abbbbc"
DB<2> s/x*y*z*/---/
DB<3> print
---Code: abbbbc
```

As you can see, it matched the "zero x, y, and z characters" at the beginning of the string.

Important Pattern Matching Rule   By default, pattern matching is from left to right. The first part from the left of the string that matches is the one that is used, even if a "larger" match occurs later in the string.

Even if you had a bunch of "x", "y", and "z" characters, they probably won't match a pattern like this:

```
DB<1> $_="Code: xxxxyyyyyzzzz"
DB<2> s/x*y*z*/---/
DB<3> print
---Code: xxxxyyyyyzzzz
```

Why did the substitution not match all those "x", "y", and "z" characters? Because pattern matching works from left to right in the string. Once the match is found, the substitution is performed.

You might think that the "g" modifier would solve the problem, but in this case it makes it even worse:

```
DB<1> $_="Code: xxxxyyyyyzzzz"
DB<2> s/x*y*z*/---/g
DB<3> print
---C---o---d---e---:--- ------
```

Even worse! EVERY occurrence of the pattern is matched and replaced. Important bit of advice: Use "+" is all cases unless you really mean to match "zero or more" of a character. The "+" character is much more likely to match what you want:

```
DB<1> $_="Code: xxxxyyyyyzzzz"
DB<2> s/x+y+z+/---/
DB<3> print
Code: ---
```

"{ }" Examples

In some cases you don't want to match "zero or more" or "one or more," but rather a specific number of repeating characters. This is what the curly braces are used for. Here are some examples:

```
DB<1> $_="Code: abccccccc"
DB<2> s/abc{1,3}/---/          #match "ab" followed by between 1-3 "c"
DB<3> print
Code: ---ccc
DB<4> $_="Code: abccccccc"
DB<5> s/abc{3,}/---/           #match "ab" followed by 3 or more "c"
DB<6> print
Code: ---
DB<7> $_="Code: abccccccc"
DB<8> s/abc{3}/---/            #match "ab" followed exactly 3 "c"
DB<9> print
Code: ---ccc
```

Important Pattern Matching Rule   Extra characters in the string "don't count." For example, if you try to use the pattern /c{1,3}/ and the string is "abccccc," the extra "c" characters at the end of the string have no impact on the match.

While it seems that the substitution of line #2 from the previous output does the same thing as line #8, there is a difference:

```
DB<1> $_="Code: abcc"
DB<2> s/abc{1,3}/---/
DB<3> print
Code: ---
DB<4> $_="Code: abcc"
DB<5> s/abc{3}/---/
DB<6> print
Code: abcc
```

Pattern Matching Is Greedy

Consider the following more closely:

```
DB<1> $_="Code: abccccc"
DB<2> s/abc{1,3}/---/          #match "ab" followed by between 1-3 "c"
DB<3> print
Code: ---ccc
```

In the preceding example, you may wonder "why did the pattern /abc{1,3}/ match three 'c' characters and not just one?". The reason is because pattern matching is greedy. Whenever possible, pattern matching will match the largest possible pattern, as long as it is still the first pattern from the left side of the string.

Important Pattern Matching Rule   Pattern matching is greedy by default. When a match is made, Perl will continue to look past the match to see if more characters can match. If so, then these other characters are included in the match.

TRY IT!

Execute the following command to enter the Perl debugger:

```
perl -d -e "1;"
```

Execute the following commands in the Perl debugger to practice the "*", "+", and curly brace metacharacters:

```
$_="#err 127 -----#err 127-----  ---#err 127---";
s/-*#err 127-*/ERROR/;
print;
$_="#err 127 -----#err 127-----  ---#err 127---";
s/-+#err 127-+/ERROR/;
print;
$_="#err 127 -----#err 127-----  ---#err 127---";
s/-{3}#err 127-{3}/ERROR/;
print;
```

Exit the Perl debugger by executing the following debugger command:

```
q
```

"." Examples

The "." character matched exactly one character. Some examples are as follows:

```
DB<1> $_="Code: A127Z"
DB<2> if (m/A...Z/) {print "yes";}
```
yes
```
DB<3> if (m/A..Z/) {print "yes";}
DB<4> if (m/A....Z/) {print "yes";}
```

Each "." must match exactly one character, no more no less.

The repeating characters ("*", "+", and curly braces) can be used in conjunction with the "." character. The following will match an "A", followed by any number one or more of "any characters," followed by a "Z":

```
DB<1> $_="Code: A127Z"
DB<2> if (m/A.+Z/) {print "yes";}
```
yes

Important Pattern Matching Rule   The "." character will match any single character EXCEPT a newline character. To include matching a newline character, use the /s modifier.

"[ ]" Examples

The square brackets are used to match a single character, but unlike the "." character, they only match a subset of characters (not any character). For example, the following will match an "A", followed by any three numbers, followed by a "Z":

```
DB<1> $_="Code: A127Z"
DB<2> if (m/A[0123456789][0123456789][0123456789]Z/) {print "yes";}
```
yes
```
DB<3> if (m/A[0-9][0-9][0-9]Z/) {print "yes";}
```
yes
```
DB<4> if (m/A[0-9]{3}Z/) {print "yes";}
```
yes

The technique used on line #3 demonstrates using a range. This range must be in the same order as the characters found in the ASCII text table.

You can also use square brackets to say "match all BUT these characters." For example, the following matches a non-numeric character, followed by three numbers, followed by a non-numeric character:

```
DB<1> $_="Code: A127Z"
DB<2> if (m/[^0-9][0-9]{3}[^0-9]/) {print "yes";}
```
yes

The ^ character means "match any but these characters." It must be the first character within the square brackets for it to mean "not these characters."

 TRY IT!

Execute the following command to enter the Perl debugger:

```
perl -d -e "1;"
```

Execute the following commands in the Perl debugger to practice the "*", "+", and curly brace metacharacters:

```
$_="#err 127 -----#err 127-----   ---#err 127---";
s/-*#err 127-*/ERROR/;
print;
$_="#err 127 -----#err 127-----   ---#err 127---";
s/-+#err 127-+/ERROR/;
print;
$_="#err 127 -----#err 127-----   ---#err 127---";
s/-{3}#err 127-{3}/ERROR/;
print;
```

Exit the Perl debugger by executing the following debugger command:

```
q
```

"?" Examples

The "?" character will make the previous character an "optional match." The character can either be there or not be there. For example:

```
DB<1> $_="In the US it is color"
DB<2> if (m/colou?r/) {print "yes";}
```
yes
```
DB<3> $_="In the UK it is colour"
DB<4> if (m/colou?r/) {print "yes";}
```
yes

"^" and "$" Examples

The "^" character will allow you to specify that you want the match to occur only at the beginning of the string, while the "$" character will allow you to specify that you want the match to occur only at the end of the string. For example:

```
DB<1> $_="This is a good day to learn Perl"
DB<2> if (/^This/) {print "yes";}
yes
DB<3> if (/This$/) {print "yes";}
DB<4> if (/^Perl/) {print "yes";}
DB<5> if (/Perl$/) {print "yes";}
yes
```

 TRY IT!

Execute the following command to enter the Perl debugger:

```
perl -d -e "1;"
```

Execute the following commands in the Perl debugger to practice the "?", "^", and "$" metacharacters:

```
$str1="It was in July that we won the war";
$str2="It was in Jul that we won the war";
if ($str1 =~ m/July?/) {print "yes";};
if ($str2 =~ m/July?/) {print "yes";};
if ($str1 =~ m/won/) {print "yes";};
if ($str1 =~ m/^won/) {print "yes";};
if ($str1 =~ m/^It/) {print "yes";};
if ($str1 =~ m/won$/) {print "yes";};
if ($str1 =~ m/war$/) {print "yes";};
```

Exit the Perl debugger by executing the following debugger command:

```
q
```

"( )" Examples

The parenthesis characters have multiple features. The first thing they do is allow you to group characters together in order to have the repeating patterns affect a group of characters rather than a single character:

```
DB<1> $_="Code: -A1CA9CA8C-"
DB<2> if (m/-(A[0-9]C){3}-/) {print "yes";}
```
yes

In the pattern on line #2, {3} repeats the previous group (A[0-9]C) three times. Without the parentheses, {3} would only apply to the previous character.

The parentheses also affects the "or" pattern character (see the next section) and also for a process called "backreferencing" that will be covered in a later section of this chapter.

"|" Examples

The "|" character allows you to specify "either or". For example, the following will match either "A1237Z" or "B999Y":

```
DB<1> $_="Code: A127Z"
DB<2> if (m/A127Z|B999Y/) {print "yes";}
```
yes
```
DB<3> $_="Code: B999Y"
DB<4> if (m/A127Z|B999Y/) {print "yes";}
```
yes

The "|" character means "match everything on one side of the | or the other side." So, the following will match either "Code: A127Z" or "B999Y" or "T888G":

```
DB<1> $_="Code: A127Z"
DB<2> if (m/Code: A127Z|B999Y|T888G/) {print "yes";}
```
yes

But, what if you wanted the "Code: " to be matched in each case? Use parentheses to limit the scope of the "or" pattern:

```
DB<1> $_="Code: A127Z"
DB<2> if (m/Code: (A127Z|B999Y|T888G)/) {print "yes";}
yes
```

"\" Examples

If you want to literally match any of the special pattern matching characters that have been covered in this chapter, like "*", ".", or "|", you need to "escape" the special character by placing the "\" character in front of it. For example, the following attempted pattern match will fail because of the improper combination of pattern matching characters:

```
DB<1> $_="Code: A+*.Z"
DB<2> if (/A+*.Z/) {print "yes";}
Nested quantifiers in regex; marked by <-- HERE in m/A+* <-- HERE .Z/ at
(eval1)[C:/Perl64/lib/perl5db.pl:646] line 2.  at (eval 11)[C:/Perl64/lib/
perl5db.pl:646] line 2.
        eval '($@, $!, $^E, $,, $/, $\\, $^W) = @saved;package main; $^D =
        $^D | $DB::db_stop;
if (/A+*.Z/) {print "yes";};

;' called at C:/Perl64/lib/perl5db.pl line 646
        DB::eval called at C:/Perl64/lib/perl5db.pl line 3244
        DB::DB called at -e line 1
```

The following example will correctly match "+" followed by "*", followed by ".":

```
DB<1> $_="Code: A+*.Z"
DB<2> if (/A\+\*\.Z/) {print "yes";}
yes
```

TRY IT!

Execute the following command to enter the Perl debugger:

```
perl -d -e "1;"
```

Execute the following commands in the Perl debugger to practice the "/", "|", and parentheses metacharacters:

```
$str1="Name: Bob";
$str2="Person: Sue";
if ($str1 =~ m/Bob|Sue/) {print "yes";};
if ($str2 =~ m/Bob|Sue/) {print "yes";};
if ($str1 =~ m/Name: Bob|Sue/) {print "yes";};
if ($str2 =~ m/Name: Bob|Sue/) {print "yes";};
if ($str1 =~ m/Name: (Bob|Sue)/) {print "yes";};
if ($str2 =~ m/Name: (Bob|Sue)/) {print "yes";};
$_="Enter this to disarm the system: ^a+\$";
if (m/^s+$/) {print "yes";};
if (m/\^s\+\$/) {print "yes";};
```

Exit the Perl debugger by executing the following debugger command:

```
q
```

Regular Expressions: Classes

Perl has some other built-in regular expressions, often called classes:

Class	Matches
\w	Alphanumeric and underscore characters
\d	Numeric
\s	White space (space, tab, newline, formfeed, return)
\b	Word boundary (includes "white space," end/beginning of line, punctuation, etc.)
\W	Non-alphanumeric and underscore characters

Class	Matches
\D	Non-numeric characters
\S	Non-white space
\B	Non-word boundary

Each of these classes represents one character:

```
if ($var =~ /^\s\w\w\w\s$/) {print "found it\n";}
```

The preceding pattern means "the first character is white space, the next three are alphanumeric (or underscore), and the last character is "white space"."

\s vs \b

The difference between \s and \b is sometimes difficult to "see." To understand the difference, we should look at why \s and \b are important to know. Take the following examples:

```
  DB<1> $_="This\tis a good day to learn Perl"
  DB<2> print
This    is a good day to learn Perl
  DB<3> s/ is / was /
  DB<4> print
This    is a good day to learn Perl
  DB<5> s/\sis\s/ was /
  DB<6> print
This was a good day to learn Perl
```

Note that " is " didn't match. If you try to match " ", it will not match a tab character. However, \s will match " " or a tab character (or other white space characters).

Programmers typically use \s to help them match words in a string. However, \s has two drawbacks when used for this purpose: (1) The white space that is matched is also replaced. (2) While white space is often the surrounding characters of a word, other things (such as the beginning and end of the string and punctuation) can surround words as well.

To overcome the shortcomings of \s, use \b. For example, to keep the "word boundary" character, you could do the following:

```
DB<1> $_="This\tis a good day to learn Perl"
DB<2> s/\bis\b/was/
DB<3> print
This     was a good day to learn Perl
```

The reason why the tab character isn't "replaced" is that \b is an assertion. An assertion is saying "what I am looking for must be in the string, but don't replace it." Anything matched with \b will not be replaced.

You can also match the beginning and end of strings with \b, as well as match other "word boundaries," such as punctuation characters:

```
DB<1> $_="is this fun?"
DB<2> s/\bis\b/was/
DB<3> print
was this fun?
DB<4> $_="This is fun."
DB<5> s/\bfun\b/great/
DB<6> print
This is great.
```

Keep in mind, \s is still useful to know. Sometimes you just want to match a white space character, not a word boundary. But, if you are trying to match a word, then \b will most likely be a better way to go.

POSIX Character Classes

Perl also supports POSIX character classes. This includes the following:

Class	Meaning
[:alnum:]	Alphanumeric characters
[:alpha:]	Alphabetic characters
[:ascii:]	ASCII characters
[:blank:]	Space and tab

Class	Meaning
[:cntrl:]	Control characters
[:digit:]	Digits
[:graph:]	Visible characters (i.e., anything except spaces, control characters, etc.)
[:lower:]	Lowercase letters
[:print:]	Visible characters and spaces (i.e., anything except control characters, etc.)
[:punct:]	Punctuation and symbols.
[:space:]	All whitespace characters, including line breaks
[:upper:]	Uppercase letters
[:word:]	Word characters (letters, numbers, and underscores)
[:xdigit:]	Hexadecimal digits

Typically, it is easier to use the previously mentioned character classes or traditional square bracket ranges. However, consider the advantage of using the [:punct:] POSIX class.

To use a POSIX class by itself, use this syntax:

```
DB<1> $string="Hello there."
DB<2> if ($string =~ m/there[[:punct:]]/) {print "yes";}
yes
```

While the POSIX standard only requires one set of square brackets, to implement this within Perl, a second set of square brackets are required. This provides the functionality of being able to combine POSIX classes with other characters, such as the following:

```
[abc[:punct:]xyz]
```

In the previous example, the RE would match a single character that was either "a", "b", "c", "x", "y", "z" or a punctuation character.

TRY IT!

Execute the following command to enter the Perl debugger:

```
perl -d -e "1;"
```

Execute the following commands in the Perl debugger to practice using the character classes:

```
$_="Code: A127Z";
if (m/Code:\s[[:upper:]]\d{3}[[:upper:]]/) {print "yes";};
if (m/Code:\s[A-Z][[:digit:]]{3}[A-Z]/) {print "yes";};
```

Exit the Perl debugger by executing the following debugger command:

```
q
```

Regular Expressions: Backreferencing

As we saw earlier, grouping (parentheses) can be used to group characters. This is primarily used to have a regular expression affect a string of characters instead of just one.

Grouping can also be used to "backreference" patterns that have been matched. When Perl makes a match of characters within parentheses, what was matched can be referred back to by a designator "\" followed by a numeric value:

```
$var =~ s/^(...)abc\1/;
```

\1 means "match what was matched in the first group," and \2 would mean "match what was matched in the second group."

In addition to being able to backreference within the regular expression, Perl assigns what was matched within the grouping to special variables. The first group matched is assigned to **$1**, the second group matched is assigned to **$2**, etc.:

```
$var =~ m/(abc..)/;
print $1;
```

This will match the string "abc" followed by the next two characters and assign all five characters to the string **$1**.

Note   If you attempt another regular expression pattern match, **$1**, **$2**...will be overwritten.

Backreferencing Example #1

In the following example, the user is asked to enter their first and last name. The first name matches the first group of parenthesis and is assigned to the **$1** variable. The last name matches the second group of parenthesis and is assigned to the **$2** variable:

```
#!perl
#9_back1.pl

print "Please enter your first and last name: ";
$_=<STDIN>;

if (m/(.*) (.*)/)  #ex: "Bob Smith"
{
print "$2, $1\n";
}
```

TRY IT!

Execute the following command to see a demonstration of backreferencing:

```
perl 9_back1.pl
```

When prompted for a name, enter the following:

```
Bob Smith
```

Backreferencing Example #2

In this example, the **group** file is read one line at a time. Each line of this file contains four fields of data separated by colons (see the following sample lines). Using the following pattern, the first field is assigned to **$1**, the second field is assigned to **$2**, etc.

```perl
#!perl
#9_back2.pl

open (GROUP, "<group");

while (<GROUP>) {
   m/(.*):(.*):(.*):(.*)/;
   $total += $3;
}

print "Total: $total\n";
```

First few lines of a typical **group** file:

```
root::0:root
other::1:
bin::2:root,bin,daemon
```

 TRY IT!

Execute the following command to see a demonstration of backreferencing:

```
perl 9_back2.pl
```

Review the results and determine if they were what you expected based on what you learned in the last section.

Backreferencing Example #3

This example illustrates two backreferencing "features." The first is that within the pattern itself, you can't use the $*num* variables because they aren't created until after the match has been successfully made. You can, however, backreference within the pattern by using *num*.

The second feature shown is that all of the *$num* variables are "wiped out" if another successful pattern match occurs.

```perl
#!perl
#9_back3.pl

print "Please enter a line: ";
$_=<STDIN>;
chomp $_;

if (/^(...).*\1$/) {print "$1\n";}

$junk="whatever";

if ($junk =~ /what/) {print "yes\n";}

print "$1\n";
```

 TRY IT!

Execute the following command to see a demonstration of backreferencing:

```
perl 9_back3.pl
```

Review the results and determine if they were what you expected based on what you learned in the last section.

Additional Resources

In each chapter, resources are provided to provide the learner with a source for more information. These resources may include downloadable source code or links to other books or articles that will provide you more information about the topic at hand.

Resources for this chapter can be found here:

https://github.com/Apress/beginning-perl-programming

Lab Exercises

Important Note   If you did not finish the previous lab, either finish it before starting this lab or use the completed cb8.pl provided in the lab answers folder.

Edit the file called cb8.pl and perform the following enhancements (save the changes into a file called cb9.pl):

- Using regular expressions, perform error checking on the following for options 1-3 to make sure the format of the date the user inputs is accurate (12/01/2019).

- Write the code for option #6 (print a statement). This option should print out all of the transactions. Use a format statement to make the output "nice." Also have it print out a total balance.

When you have completed your work, compare your script against the cb9.pl file provided in lab answers.

CHAPTER 10

Perl Utilities

split

The **split** statement is useful for breaking up a scalar value based on a particular character (or characters). It will return what is split as a list (array) of scalar values. This list is normally assigned to an array:

```
DB<1> $str = "Bob:Jones:23423:manager:03"
DB<2> @fields=split(/:/, $str)
DB<3> for $item (@fields) {print $i++, " $item\n";}
0 Bob
1 Jones
2 23423
3 manager
4 03
```

Note   /:/ is actually a regular expression pattern.

Using $_

If the variable you are splitting is **$_**, you don't need to specify the variable name; **split** will assume you want to split **$_**:

```
DB<1> $_ = "Bob:Jones:23423:manager:03"
DB<2> @fields=split(/:/)
DB<3> for $item (@fields) {print $i++, " $item\n";}
0 Bob
1 Jones
```

© William "Bo" Rothwell of One Course Source, Inc. 2019
W. "Bo" Rothwell, *Beginning Perl Programming*, https://doi.org/10.1007/978-1-4842-5055-6_10

2 23423

3 manager

4 03

Using Regular Expressions with split

It's common to split a variable based on one or more occurrences of white space. If you want to do this, you can use the **\s+** regular expression:

```
DB<1> $_="Today is Monday"
DB<2> @fields=split(/\s+/, $_)
DB<3> for $item (@fields) {print $i++, " $item\n";}
```

0 Today

1 is

2 Monday

Since splitting of "white space plus" is so common, it is the default pattern for the **split** command. Which means that if you are splitting **$_** on **\s+**, you can use the following:

```
DB<1> $_="Today is Monday"
DB<2> @fields=split
DB<3> for $item (@fields) {print $i++, " $item\n";}
```

0 Today

1 is

2 Monday

Limit the Output of split

You can specify a third parameter to limit the number of values that split returns. For example, to return the first three fields of the string, execute the following:

```
DB<1> $_ = "Bob:Jones:23423:manager:03"
DB<2> @fields=split(/:/, $_, 3)
DB<3> for $item (@fields) {print $i++, " $item\n";}
```

0 Bob

1 Jones

2 23423:manager:03

TRY IT!

Execute the following command to enter the Perl debugger:

```
perl -d -e "1;"
```

Execute the following commands in the Perl debugger to practice using the split statement:

```
$_="Steve+Bob+Nick+Tom+Sue+Tim+Nick";
@people=split(/\+/, $_);
print $people[0];
($name1, $name2)=split(/\+/);
print $name1;
print $name2;
```

Exit the Perl debugger by executing the following debugger command:

```
q
```

join

The **join** statement can be used to combine scalar values (or scalar variables, or elements in an array) into a single scalar value (or variable):

```
DB<1> $_ = "Bob:Jones:23423:manager:03"
DB<2> @fields=split(/:/, $_)
DB<3> for $item (@fields) {print $i++, " $item\n";}
0 Bob
1 Jones
2 23423
3 manager
4 03
DB<4> $str=join("~", @fields)
DB<5> print $str
Bob~Jones~23423~manager~03
```

Notes:

- The first parameter to the **join** statement is the character(s) to join with.

- The additional parameters are what to join. If an array is specified, all of the elements in the array are joined. Separate scalars values (or variables) can be specified:

```
$str = join("~", "abc", "xyz", "123")
```

substr

The **substr** statement returns the character(s) in a string when given a position range. For example, if you want the 6th–9th characters of a string, the following code will "grab" those characters:

```
DB<1> $str="This is a good time to learn Perl"
DB<2> print substr ($str, 5, 4)
is a
```

Notes:

- The first parameter of the **substr** statement is the variable to "look in."

- The second parameter is the starting point. This is always indexed from 0.

- The third parameter is how many characters to grab.

If the third parameter is omitted, then **substr** will grab all of the remaining characters:

```
DB<1> $str="This is a good time to learn Perl"
DB<2> print substr ($str, 5)
is a good time to learn Perl
```

You can also index from the back of the string with negative numbers:

```
DB<1> $str="This is a good time to learn Perl"
DB<2> print substr ($str, -7, 4)
rn P
```

You can use **substr** to modify a variable as well as return characters from the variable:

```
DB<1> $str="This is a good time to learn Perl"
DB<2> substr ($str, -4, 4)="how to program"
DB<3> print $str
```
This is a good time to learn how to program

or:

```
DB<1> $str="This is a good time to learn Perl"
DB<2> substr ($str, -4, 4, "how to program")
DB<3> print $str
```
This is a good time to learn how to program

 TRY IT!

Execute the following command to enter the Perl debugger:

```
perl -d -e "1;"
```

Execute the following commands in the Perl debugger to practice using the substr statement:

```
$_="It was the best of times, it was the worst of times…";
print substr ($_, 7, 8);
print substr ($_, 7);
substr ($_, -21) = "a very good year!";
print;
```

Exit the Perl debugger by executing the following debugger command:

```
q
```

index

The **index** statement will search for a sub-string within another string and return the index position of the sub-string found:

```
DB<1> $str="This is a good time to learn Perl"
DB<2> print index ($str, "good")
```
10

Notes:

- The number returned is indexed from 0.

- The number returned is where the first character of the sub-string was found.

You can also skip past characters and start the search later in the string:

```
DB<1> $str="This is a good time to learn Perl"
DB<2> print index ($str, "i", 8)
```
16

Notes:

- If the sub-string isn't found in the string, index returns -1.

- To search from the back of the string, use the **rindex** statement (next section).

rindex

The **rindex** statement will search a string from the back and return the index position of the sub-string found:

```
DB<1> $str="This is a good time to learn Perl"
DB<2> print rindex ($str, "i")
```
16

Notes:

- The number returned is indexed from 0 *from the front of the string*.

158

TRY IT!

Execute the following command to enter the Perl debugger:

```
perl -d -e "1;"
```

Execute the following commands in the Perl debugger to practice using the index and rindex statements:

```
$_="It was the best of times, it was the worst of times…";
print index ($_, "the");
print index ($_, "the", 8);
$position = rindex ($_,"of");
```

Exit the Perl debugger by executing the following debugger command:

```
q
```

grep

While regular expressions pattern matching works well with strings, it's a bit of a pain for elements in an array. The **grep** statement will look at each element of an array and return those that match the expression:

```
#!perl
#10_grep.pl

@array=qw(Bob Bobby Ted Fred Sue Nick Sally);
@b=grep (/^B/, @array);
print "@b";
```

 TRY IT!

Execute the following command to see a demonstration of the grep statement:

```
perl 10_grep.pl
```

Review the results and determine if they were what you expected based on what you learned in the last section.

srand and rand

The **srand** and **rand** statements are used to generate random numbers. Since computers can't generate truly random numbers, an algorithm is used to create a random number. This algorithm uses a "seed" (a starting *integer* number for the algorithm). To set the seed, use the **srand** statement:

```
srand(12345);
```

Of course, if the same starting seed (number) is used over and over, the "random" number will always be the same. Since the **time** statement returns an integer number that is different from one second to another, it's output is normally used to set the seed:

```
srand(time);
```

The **rand** statement creates the random number using the seed. It accepts an integer at its argument:

```
$num=rand(10);    #generate a random number from 0 to 9.99999
```

To make this floating point number an integer, use the **int** statement:

```
$num=int(rand(10));   #generates a random number from 0 to 9
```

The **int** statement always rounds down; to generate a random number from 1 to 10, just add 1 to the result:

```
$num = int(rand(10)) +1;
```

 TRY IT!

Execute the following command to enter the Perl debugger:

```
perl -d -e "1;"
```

Execute the following command in the Perl debugger repeatedly until it is clear to you that the output of each command is between 0 and 5 (but not including the value of 5):

```
print rand(5);
```

Execute the following command in the Perl debugger repeatedly until it is clear to you that the output of each command is either 0, 1, 2, 3, or 4:

```
print int (rand(5));
```

Execute the following command in the Perl debugger repeatedly until it is clear to you that the output of each command is either 1, 2, 3, 4, or 5:

```
print int (rand(5)) +1;
```

Exit the Perl debugger by executing the following debugger command:

```
q
```

sleep

The **sleep** statement is useful for "pausing" your program for a set amount of time (in seconds). For example, the following program will perform a "countdown" from 10 to 1:

```perl
#!perl
#10_sleep.pl

print "countdown!\n\n";
$|=1;
for ($i=10;$i>0;$i--) {
    print "$i \r";
    sleep 1;
}
$|=0;
print "Blast off!\n";
```

Notes:

- You can only pass integers to the **sleep** statement.

- Actual "sleep time" will very due to the system clock accuracy and system load.

- The **$|=1** statement tells Perl to flush the STDOUT buffer whenever data is sent to STDOUT. Typically, the output buffer is flushed only when certain events take place (a newline is sent to STDOUT, and STDIN is read from or the end of the program).

TRY IT!

Execute the following command to see a demonstration of the sleep statement:

`perl 10_sleep.pl`

Review the results and determine if they were what you expected based on what you learned in the last section.

Modify the 10_sleep.pl file by commenting out the line "$|=1;". Execute the command again. You should not see any output on the screen besides "countdown" and "Blast off!". Look at the notes from the previous section to determine why this is.

Additional Resources

In each chapter, resources are provided to provide the learner with a source for more information. These resources may include downloadable source code or links to other books or articles that will provide you more information about the topic at hand.

Resources for this chapter can be found here:

`https://github.com/Apress/beginning-perl-programming`

Lab Exercises

Important Note   If you did not finish the previous lab, either finish it before starting this lab or use the completed cb9.pl provided in the lab answers folder.

Edit the file called cb9.pl and perform the following enhancements (save the changes into a file called cb10.pl):

- Modify the code that you created in the previous chapter lab that computed the total balance. Use split instead of regular expressions to manipulate the data when you open the file and read its contents.

- Write the code for option #4 (look up check by number). Perform error checking as needed.

When you have completed your work, compare your script against the cb9.pl file provided in lab answers.

CHAPTER 11

Filesystem and Process Control

Controlling the Filesystem Within Perl

Perl provides several built-in statements that allow you to control the filesystem (files and directories) while within Perl. With these statements, you can

- Change directories
- List files
- Make directories
- Remove directories
- Remove files
- Rename files
- Make links (not covered in this chapter)
- Change permissions
- Get information regarding a file

Perl also allows you to run operating system (OS) commands from within your Perl script. Most operating systems provide commands that allow you to modify the filesystem. These commands, such as **mkdir** and **ls**, are the methods the OS user uses to manipulate files and directories.

© William "Bo" Rothwell of One Course Source, Inc. 2019
W. "Bo" Rothwell, *Beginning Perl Programming*, https://doi.org/10.1007/978-1-4842-5055-6_11

Avoid Running Operating System Commands

Running OS commands can result in several "problems":

- Your Perl script may run slower. The reason for this is that Perl must spawn another process (e.g., a UNIX/Linux shell) to run the OS command.

- Your script may become "platform dependant" as the OS command that you attempt to run may not be available on another operating system.

- Your script may become "user dependant." A user can modify his/her environment (such as aliases, functions, and the PATH variable) to alter the way that OS commands execute. If they do, this may cause problems when you run these OS commands from within your Perl script.

Working with Directories

Perl knows what directory the user was in when the script was started. To have Perl display this information, run the OS command that lists the current working directory by using the **system** statement. To move to a different directory, use the **chdir** statement:

```
  DB<1> system "pwd"
/root
  DB<2> chdir ("/etc")
  DB<3> system "pwd"
/etc
  DB<4> chdir ("..")
  DB<5> system "pwd"
/
```

Notes:

- The directory name MUST be in quotes: "/etc/skel".

- When your Perl script exits, the user is in the directory that he/she started from. Your Perl script can't change the directory in the shell the user ran the program from.

Listing Files

To list files in a directory, use Perl's wildcard file naming convention. By placing angled brackets around the wildcards, Perl will return a list of all of the files that match the wildcard pattern. This list is most often either assigned to a variable or used as a variable:

```
@files=(</etc/s*>);        #Assigns all of the files in the /etc directory
                           that start with
                           #the letter "s" to the @files array

chdir("/etc");
@files=(<s*>);             #Same as above using relative pathnames

foreach $file (</etc/s*>) {
   print "$file\n";        #print each file a line at a time
}
```

Multiple wild card patterns are allowed:

```
@files=(</etc/s*  /usr/bin/s*>);
```

Making Directories

To make a directory, use the **mkdir** statement:

```
mkdir("/tmp/data", 0755);
```

The first parameter passed into the **mkdir** statement is the name of the directory to create. The second parameter is the permissions to set on that directory. This number has to be given as an octal value. That is why the leading "0" exists.

UNIX and Linux provide users with a feature called *umask*, a method of setting default permissions so that all new files and directories are created with the same set of permissions each time. Unfortunately, when Perl creates a directory, the umask setting is imposed upon Perl. Therefore, if the user has a more restrictive umask than the permissions you are trying to create for the directory, the umask wins and the permissions aren't what you wanted them to be.

Set the permissions manually after the **mkdir** statement with the **chmod** statement (see the next section) to overcome this potential problem.

Notes:

- On non-UNIX systems, the permission argument is ignored.

- Prior to Perl 5.6, the permission argument is required for UNIX and Linux systems. In Perl 5.6 and higher, if no permission argument is provided, Perl uses the umask value of 0777.

- The **mkdir** statement returns a true value if the directory is created and a false value if the directory is not created.

Removing Directories

To delete a directory, use the **rmdir** statement:

```
rmdir ("/tmp/data");
```

Notes:

- If the directory contains files or subdirectories, the **rmdir** statement will fail (see the next section to see how to remove files).

- The **rmdir** statement will return a numeric value that indicates how many directories were deleted. Therefore, it can be used naturally in a conditional statement to determine if the command succeeded or failed.

 TRY IT!

Execute the following command to some files to work with:

```
cp /etc/*.conf .
```

Execute the following command to enter the Perl debugger:

```
perl -d -e "1;"
```

Execute the following commands in the Perl debugger to practice working with directories:

```
mkdir ("data");
chdir ("data");
system "pwd";
```

```
chdir ("..");
system "pwd";
@files=(<*>);
print ("@files");
rmdir ("data");
```

Exit the Perl debugger by executing the following debugger command:

```
q
```

Working with Files

Let's see how to work with files.

Deleting Files

Use the **unlink** statement to remove files:

```
unlink("/tmp/data_1");
unlink(</tmp/data*>);          #Using wildcards
```

Renaming Files

Perl provides the ability to rename files by using the **rename** statement:

```
rename ("/tmp/data", "/tmp/data.old");
```

Changing Permissions

The **chmod** statement will allow you to change permissions of files or directories:

```
chmod (0644, "/tmp/data");
```

Remember, the first number (0) indicates that this is an octal value.

Note   The **unlink**, **rename**, and **chmod** statements return true if the statement is successful and false if it fails.

Gathering File Information

The **stat** statement will provide an array of useful information regarding a file or directory. According to the Perl documentation, the following describes the fields that the **stat** statement returns:

Index	Value returned
0	Device number of filesystem
1	Inode number
2	File mode (type and permissions)
3	Number of (hard) links to the file
4	Numeric user ID of file's owner
5	Numeric group ID of file's owner
6	Device identifier (special files only)
7	Total size of file, in bytes
8	Last access time in seconds since the epoch
9	Last modify time in seconds since the epoch
10	Inode change time in seconds since the epoch (∗)
11	Preferred block size for filesystem I/O
12	Actual number of blocks allocated

stat example:

```
DB<1> @info=stat("/etc/hosts")
DB<2> for $i (0..12) {print "$i\t$info[$i]\n";}
0    776
1    28718
2    33188
3    1
4    0
5    0
6    0
7    177
```

8	1139268755
9	1117559373
10	1117559373
11	4096
12	2

 TRY IT!

Execute the following command to create a file to work with:

```
echo "hello" > hello.txt
```

Execute the following command to enter the Perl debugger:

```
perl -d -e "1;"
```

Execute the following commands in the Perl debugger to practice working with files:

```
@data=stat("hello.txt");
print "@data";
rename ("hello.txt", "newfile.txt");
@files=(<*.txt>);
unlink ("newfile.txt");
@files=(<*.txt>);
```

Exit the Perl debugger by executing the following debugger command:

```
q
```

Backquoting

In a previous chapter we saw how a filehandle can be opened to read the output of an OS command. While this is useful for commands that provide a large amount of output, it's cumbersome for commands that only have a line or two of output. By using backquotes, we can run an OS command and return the value to a scalar variable:

```
$date = `date`;
```

The preceding example runs the UNIX (or Linux) command **date** and returns the output of the command back to the assignment. So, the scalar variable **$date** will contain the output of the **date** command.

Other examples:

```
$pwd = `pwd`;
$top = `head /etc/group`;
$machine = `uname -n`;
$clear=`clear`;
```

Note:

- You can't use back quoting with the OS command **cls** in the Windows environment.

The system Statement

Another method of running OS commands, the **system** statement, will send the output of the OS command to the screen (as opposed to sending the output back into your Perl script). This is good for tasks like clearing the screen:

```
print "Enter your name: ";
chomp($name= <STDIN>);
system "clear";
print "Hello, $name, welcome to my script\n";
```

The only difference between the backquote method and using the **system** statement is where the output of the OS command goes. With backquotes, the output is returned to the command line itself before the Perl statement executes. The **system** statement sends its output to STDOUT.

TRY IT!

Execute the following command to enter the Perl debugger:

```
perl -d -e "1;"
```

Execute the following commands in the Perl debugger to practice running OS commands:

```
system "date";
$today=`date`;
print $today;
```

Exit the Perl debugger by executing the following debugger command:

```
q
```

Additional Resources

In each chapter, resources are provided to provide the learner with a source for more information. These resources may include downloadable source code or links to other books or articles that will provide you more information about the topic at hand.

Resources for this chapter can be found here:

```
https://github.com/Apress/beginning-perl-programming
```

Lab Exercises

Important Note   If you did not finish the previous lab, either finish it before starting this lab or use the completed cb10.pl provided in the lab answers folder.

Edit the file called cb10.pl and perform the following enhancements (save the changes into a file called cb11.pl):

- Make the data file have only read and write permissions for the owner of the file (and no permissions for anyone else) (UNIX OS only).

- Use the OS command to clear the screen when displaying the menu or whenever an option is chosen ("clear" in UNIX, "cls" in Windows).

- Write the code for option #5 (look up check by date). Perform error checking as needed.

When you have completed your work, compare your script against the cb11.pl file provided in lab answers.

CHAPTER 12

Functions

Creating Functions

To create a function, use the **sub** statement:

```
sub total {
  print "The total is ", $a * $b + $c * $d, "\n";
}
```

Notes:

- Functions are most often created for either breaking up a large script into "components" or for when code is used more than once within a script.

- Be careful when choosing function names. Perl has many built-in functions (see how to avoid confusion in the "Invoking Functions" section).

- Functions cannot be "redeclared" because they are created at compile time, not run time.

- Functions can be placed anywhere in your Perl script, even after they are called (if they are called correctly).

- By default, variables declared in your main program can be accessed and modified in your functions. More on this in the "Scope of Variables" section.

© William "Bo" Rothwell of One Course Source, Inc. 2019
W. "Bo" Rothwell, *Beginning Perl Programming*, https://doi.org/10.1007/978-1-4842-5055-6_12

Invoking Functions

To invoke (call) a function, specify the ampersand character (&) followed by the function name:

```
sub total {
  print "The total is ", $a * $b + $c * $d, "\n";
}

$a=10;
$b=20;
$c=5;
$d=2;

&total;
```

The function call doesn't really require the ampersand character. However, it is highly recommended that you place an "&" prior to function calls because of the following reasons:

1. It makes it easier for other programmers to see that this is a user-defined function that is being called.

2. If you use the name of a Perl built-in function and you **don't** use the "&" character, then the Perl built-in function will be called. If you **do** use the "&" character, then the function you created will be called.

3. If you want to put your functions after they are called in your program, using the "&" character is one of the "proper" ways to call the function.

TRY IT!

Execute the following command to enter the Perl debugger:

```
perl -d -e "1;"
```

Execute the following commands in the Perl debugger to practice creating and invoking functions:

```
sub mult {print $a * $b;};
$a=9;
$b=7;
&mult;
```

Exit the Perl debugger by executing the following debugger command:

```
q
```

Returning Values from Functions

All functions return a value to the calling program. Although this return value is normally a scalar variable, it can also be an array or an associative array.

Two methods can be used to return a value to the calling program: the explicit method and the more cryptic implied method.

The Explicit Method

With the explicit method, use the **return** statement to specify what value to return to the calling program:

```
sub total {
  $total = $a * $b + $c * $d;
  return ($total);
}
```

You can either return the value of a variable or the outcome of a Perl statement:

```
sub total {
  return ($a * $b + $c * $d);
}
```

One of the advantages of using the **return** statement is that it is clear to another programmer what is being returned. Another advantage is that you can use the **return** statement to "pop out" of a function prematurely:

```
sub test {
    if ($var =~ /ERROR/) {
        return (0);
    }
$result = $var;
chop ($result);
$result =~ s/^.../Pattern: /;
return ($result);
}
```

The Implicit Method

If you don't specify what to return with the **return** statement, Perl will return the outcome of the last statement in the function:

```
sub total {
  $a * $b + $c * $d;
}
```

In this example, the outcome of the mathematical equation is returned. While this method requires less typing, it doesn't provide any additional features and is a bit more cryptic than simply using the **return** statement.

TRY IT!

Execute the following command to enter the Perl debugger:

```
perl -d -e "1;"
```

Execute the following commands in the Perl debugger to practice returning values from functions:

```
sub mult {return ($a * $b);};
$a=9;
$b=7;
$total=&mult;
print $total;
```

Exit the Perl debugger by executing the following debugger command:

```
q
```

Passing Parameters

To pass parameters into a function, place the parameters within parentheses after the function call:

```
&average ($a, $b);
```

The variables $a and $b will be passed into the function average. Within the function you can access what was passed in by using the special array @_. The first parameter will be stored in $_[0], and the second parameter will be stored in $_[1]...:

```
sub average {
   foreach $num (@_) {
      $total += $num;
   }
return ($total / ($#_+1));
}

$a=10;
$b=20;
print &average ($a, $b);        #prints 15
```

Note:

- Just like any array, $#_ holds the last index number of @_

When you pass a parameter into a function, you actually pass a *reference*. In a sense, the elements in the **@_** array share the same memory space as the variables that were passed into the function from the main program. Changing elements in the **@_** array will also change the variable that is being passed in:

```
sub average {
   $_[0]++;                        #Adds one to first element of _ array (and $a)
   foreach $num (@_) {
      $total += $num;
   }
return ($total / ($#_+1));
}

#main program
$a=10;
$b=20;
print &average ($a, $b), "\n"; #prints 15.5
print $a;                       #prints 11
```

To avoid this, you should reassign elements in **@_** to other variables (either scalar or another array). When variables are assigned, they are assigned by *value* by default, not by *reference*:

```
sub average {
   @temp=@_;
   $temp[0]++;                     #Adds one to first element of temp array
   foreach $num (@temp) {
      $total += $num;
   }
return ($total / ($#temp+1));
}
```

```
#main program
$a=10;
$b=20;
print &average ($a, $b), "\n";        #prints 15.5
print $a;                             #prints 10
```

Warning: Don't confuse the scalar variable **$_** (the default variable) with the array variable **@_** ; They are completely different variables.

TRY IT!

Execute the following command to enter the Perl debugger:

```
perl -d -e "1;"
```

Execute the following commands in the Perl debugger to practice passing data into functions:

```
sub mult {print $_[0] * $_[1];};
$a=9;
$b=7;
&mult($a, $b);
sub mult2 {$_[0]++; print $_[0] * $_[1];};
&mult2($a, $b);
print "a is $a and b is $b\n";
sub mult3 {@input=@_; $input[0]++; print $input[0] * $input[1];}
&mult3($a, $b);
print "a is $a and b is $b\n";
```

Exit the Perl debugger by executing the following debugger command:

```
q
```

Scope of Variables

By default, almost all variables in Perl are "global" in scope. This means that any variable that you create in your main program can be accessed and modified by any function. While being able to have global variables is good for some situations, it can cause problems when you (or fellow programmers) use the same variable name for different reasons within the same script:

```perl
#!perl
#12_scope1.pl

sub average {
    @temp=@_;
    $temp[0]++;                          #Adds one to first element of temp array
    foreach $num (@temp) {
        $total += $num;
    }
return ($total / ($#temp+1));
}

#main program
@temp=(10,20);
print &average (@temp), "\n";        #prints 15.5
print "@temp";                        #prints 11, 20
```

Perl does provide two statements (**local** and **my**) that allow you to impose *scope* on a variable. The idea of scope is it limits the "availability" of a variable to a certain portion (typically a function) of your script.

TRY IT!

Execute the following command to see a demonstration of the scope of variable:

`perl 12_scope1.pl`

Review the results and determine if they were what you expected based on what you learned in the last section.

local() vs. my()
The local Statement

The **local** statement can be used to protect the calling program's variables from being modified from the function:

```perl
#!perl
#12_scope2.pl

sub average {
   local(@temp)=@_;              #Main program's @temp isn't touched
   $temp[0]++;                   #Adds one to first element of local temp array
   foreach $num (@temp) {
      $total += $num;
   }
return ($total / ($#temp+1));
}

#main program
@temp=(10,20);
print &average (@temp), "\n";    #prints 15.5
print "@temp";                   #prints 10, 20
```

In the preceding example, the **local** statement makes a variable called temp. This variable can't modify the temp variable in the main program.

TRY IT!

Execute the following command to see a demonstration of the scope of variable:

```
perl 12_scope2.pl
```

Review the results and determine if they were what you expected based on what you learned in the last section.

However, the **local** statement doesn't protect the function's variables from being changed by other functions:

```perl
#!perl
#12_scope3.pl

sub modify {
    @temp=(40,50);           #changes temp that was created in average function
}

sub average {
    local(@temp)=@_;                       #Main program's @temp isn't touched
    &modify;
    return (($temp[0] + $temp[1]) / 2);   #returns 45, result of 40 + 50 /2
}

#main program
@temp=(10,20);
print &average (@temp), "\n";            #prints 45
print "@temp";                           #prints 10, 20
```

A graphical representation:

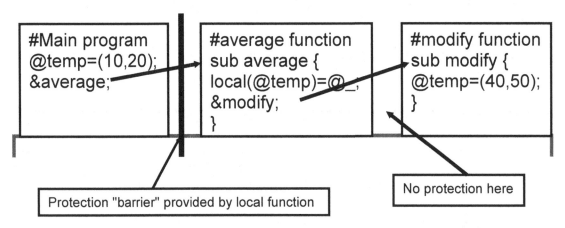

Protection "barrier" provided by local function

No protection here

Execute the following command to see a demonstration of the scope of variable:

`perl 12_scope3.pl`

Review the results and determine if they were what you expected based on what you learned in the last section.

The my Statement

The **my** statement is like the **local** statement in that it protects the calling program from having its variables modified by the function. However, **my** also protect the function from having its variable changed by another function:

```perl
#!perl
#12_scope4.pl

sub modify {
    @temp=(40,50);        #changes temp, but not the average function's temp
}

sub average {
    my(@temp)=@_;         #Main program's @temp isn't touched
    &modify;
return (($temp[0] + $temp[1]) / 2);     #returns 15
}

#main program
@temp=(10,20);
print &average (@temp), "\n";     #prints 15
print "@temp";                    #prints 40, 50
```

185

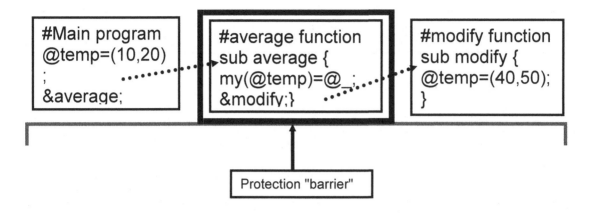

⌨🖱 **TRY IT!**

Execute the following command to see a demonstration of the scope of variable:

`perl 12_scope4.pl`

Review the results and determine if they were what you expected based on what you learned in the last section.

The bad "side affect" of this is that when the modify function assigns the **temp** variable, it ends up modifying the main program (global) **temp** variable. To avoid this, either use the **my** statement when creating the main program's variables or use the **my** statement when creating the modify function's variables (or even better, do both!):

```perl
#!perl
#12_scope5.pl

sub modify {
    my(@temp)=(40,50);          #changes the temp var of the modify function
}

sub average {
    my(@temp)=@_;               #Main program's @temp isn't touched
    &modify;
return (($temp[0] + $temp[1]) / 2);     #returns 15
}
```

```
#main program
my(@temp)=(10,20);
print &average (@temp), "\n";          #prints 15
print "@temp";                          #prints 10, 20
```

TRY IT!

Execute the following command to see a demonstration of the scope of variable:

`perl 12_scope5.pl`

Review the results and determine if they were what you expected based on what you learned in the last section.

Additional Resources

In each chapter, resources are provided to provide the learner with a source for more information. These resources may include downloadable source code or links to other books or articles that will provide you more information about the topic at hand.

Resources for this chapter can be found here:

`https://github.com/Apress/beginning-perl-programming`

Lab Exercises

Important Note   If you did not finish the previous lab, either finish it before starting this lab or use the completed cb11.pl provided in the lab answers folder.

Edit the file called cb11.pl and perform the following enhancements (save the changes into a file called cb12.pl):

- Where logical, convert your code into functions. For example, printing the menu could be one function, each menu option can be separate functions, and working with the data file (reading, opening) can be separate functions. Be sure to use **my** where appropriate.

When you have completed your work, compare your script against the cb12.pl file provided in lab answers.

CHAPTER 13

Using Modules

What Are Modules?

Perl modules (sometimes called libraries) are files that contain reusable code. These libraries can either be created by you, built-in to Perl, or downloaded from the Internet.

This chapter will focus on using built-in Perl modules. Creating your own modules and using modules that you get from the Internet are discussed in a future course.

Loading Modules with use

Typically, modules declare generic functions that can be used within your script. To make use of these functions, use the **use** statement to tell Perl to "import" the functions into your script:

```
use File::Copy;
copy("example.txt", "newfile.txt");
```

The module "File::Copy" contains a package (a namespace where functions are declared) that contains two functions: **copy** and **move**.

The "File" part of "File::Copy" indicates that the "Copy" module (really called Copy. pm) is under a directory called "File." The "File" directory is under one of the directories indicated by the elements in the **@INC** variable:

```
DB<1> print "@INC"
/usr/local/lib/perl5/5.00503/sun4-solaris /usr/local/lib/perl5/5.00503 /
usr/local/lib/perl5/site_perl/5.005/sun4-solaris /usr/local/lib/perl5/site_
perl/5.005 .
```

Perl has many built-in modules which can be used with your script. To see a list of them, run the command "man perlmodlib" and search for "Standard Modules."

© William "Bo" Rothwell of One Course Source, Inc. 2019
W. "Bo" Rothwell, *Beginning Perl Programming*, https://doi.org/10.1007/978-1-4842-5055-6_13

 TRY IT!

Execute the following command to enter the Perl debugger:

```
perl -d -e "1;"
```

Execute the following commands in the Perl debugger to practice loading and using modules:

```
use Text::Wrap;
$line="The Text::Wrap module provides a function called wrap which is
designed to provide you with a better way to display (print) output
to a filehandle (normally it is used to print to the screen.  It does
'work wrapping', a feature not provided by the print statement.  See the
documentation for more details.";
print $line;
print wrap("\t", "", $line);
```

Exit the Perl debugger by executing the following debugger command:

```
q
```

Other Functions of use

The **use** statement can also be used to modify the behavior of your Perl script. The following examples are some of the common methods of using **use** to modify the behavior of your script:

Command	Meaning
use diagnostics	Force verbose warning diagnostics
use strict	Restrict unsafe constructs (see variations and details in the following)

use diagnostics

This statement is very useful when debugging programs consider the following code:

```
#!perl
```

#13_diag.pl

```
use diagnostics;
print "this is only a test;
```

There is a syntax error (no ending quotes) which typically produces the following compiler error:

```
Can't find string terminator ' " ' anywhere before EOF at 13_diag.pl line 2
```

When run when diagnostics are "turned on," the following error is displayed:

```
Can't find string terminator ' " ' anywhere before EOF at 13_diag.pl line 2

    (F) Perl strings can stretch over multiple lines.  This message means
    that
    the closing delimiter was omitted.   Because bracketed quotes count
    nesting
    levels, the following is missing its final parenthesis:

        print q(The character '(' starts a side comment.);
```

Note: remaining output omitted

use strict

There are three things you can tell Perl to be strict about: reference usage, subroutine usage, and variable usage.

use strict 'ref'

This will cause your program to exit if a symbolic reference is used. Symbolic references are a method of referring to variable and are typically discussed in advanced classes.

use strict 'vars'

This will generate an error if a variable used hasn't been either declared as a **my** variable or isn't fully qualified. A fully qualified variable is one that includes its package namespace in the variable name. Packages are discussed in advanced Perl classes.

use strict 'subs'

This pragma will generate an error message for if you attempt to use "barewords" (a string that doesn't have quotes around it) that attempts to call a subroutine that hasn't been declared. For example:

```perl
#!perl
#13_subs.pl

use strict 'subs';

sub jesttest {
  print "This is just a test";
}

sub hello {
print "hello\n";
}

hello;     #Calls a valid subroutine, no problem
justatest; #Bareword that isn't a subroutine.
```

Note   The statement **use strict** will enforce all restrictions (refs, subs, and vars).

TRY IT!

Execute the following command to see a demonstration of the scope of variable:

```
perl 13_subs.pl
```

Review the results and determine if they were what you expected based on what you learned in the last section.

Additional Resources

In each chapter, resources are provided to provide the learner with a source for more information. These resources may include downloadable source code or links to other books or articles that will provide you more information about the topic at hand.

Resources for this chapter can be found here:

```
https://github.com/Apress/beginning-perl-programming
```

Lab Exercises

Important Note   If you did not finish the previous lab, either finish it before starting this lab or use the completed cb12.pl provided in the lab answers folder.

Edit the file called cb12.pl and perform the following enhancements (save the changes into a file called cb13.pl):

- When opening a data file, first make a backup copy of the file. The name should be "*person*.data.bak" where person is the name of the person running the program. Inform the user of this backup file.

- Implement **use diagnostics**.

- Implement **use strict "subs"**.

When you have completed your work, compare your script against the cb13.pl file provided in lab answers.

Debugging Perl

The -w Switch

The **-w** switch (option) will tell Perl to look for and report unusual code. This code typically includes a logical (not syntax) error and includes (but not excluded to) the following:

- Variable names that are mentioned only once

- Scalar variables that are set before use

- Redefined subroutines

- References to undefined filehandles

- References to filehandles opened read-only that the script is attempting to write to

- Values used as a number that don't look like numbers

- Arrays used in scalar context

- Subroutines that "recurse" more than 100 deep

Using the **-w** switch can avoid common (but sometimes tricky) programming errors such as the ones demonstrated in the following program:

```perl
#!perl
#14_w.pl

if ($var == 0) {
  print "yes\n";
}
```

© William "Bo" Rothwell of One Course Source, Inc. 2019
W. "Bo" Rothwell, *Beginning Perl Programming*, https://doi.org/10.1007/978-1-4842-5055-6_14

```
print GROUP "hello there\n";

$name="Bob";

if ($name == "Ted") {
    print "yes\n";
}
```

TRY IT!

Execute the following command to see a demonstration of the -w switch:

```
perl -w 14_w.pl
```

Review the results and determine if they were what you expected based on what you learned in the last section.

The Perl Debugger

Perl provides a built-in debugger which can be invoked when running Perl with the **-d** option:

```
[student@ocs student]$ perl -d example.pl
Loading DB routines from perl5db.pl version 1.0402

Enter h or 'h h' for help

main::(use.pl:2)            copy("example.txt", "newfile.txt ");
  DB<1>
```

Some notes about the debugger:

- Perl must first be able to compile the code prior to entering the debugger.

- main::(use.pl:2) means "Main part of script use.pl, line #2".

- At this point, no statements have been executed.

- The command above the prompt (DB<1>) is the next command to execute.

Debugger Commands

The debugger has many built-in commands. The most common are as follows.

Command	Meaning
!! cmd	Runs the command (cmd) in a separate process (this is typically a shell command)
h	Interactive help
H -num	Prints last "num" commands (excludes single character commands)
l	Lists the next line of code to be executed
n	Steps through a statement (if subroutines are called, executes over the subroutine)
q	Quits the debugger
s	Steps through a statement (if subroutines are called, executes one subroutine statement at a time)
V	Displays all of the variables in package (defaults to main)

In addition to the debugger commands, you can execute any Perl statement.

Additional Resources

In each chapter, resources are provided to provide the learner with a source for more information. These resources may include downloadable source code or links to other books or articles that will provide you more information about the topic at hand.

Resources for this chapter can be found here:

`https://github.com/Apress/beginning-perl-programming`

Lab Exercises

There is no lab for this chapter. As a challenge, consider making the following changes to your checkbook script:

1. Modify option #6 to print statement for the following:

    A. Just display checks

    B. Just display deposits

    C. Just display withdrawals

    D. Display transactions for a given month

    E. Display transactions for a given date

    F. Display transactions from a "start" to an "end" date

2. Add an option to allow the user to modify a transaction.

3. Allow the user to choose which directory to store the data file.

4. Add an option to allow the user to delete a transaction.

5. Perform better error checking when reading and writing from the data file. For example:

    A. If the file isn't readable by the user, but the user owns the file, change the permissions for reading for the user.

    B. The program will fail to create new files if the directory isn't writable. If this is the case, allow the user to choose a different directory to save the file.

6. Add a Save option.

Index

© William "Bo" Rothwell of One Course Source, Inc. 2019
W. "Bo" Rothwell, *Beginning Perl Programming*, https://doi.org/10.1007/978-1-4842-5055-6